Exercises in Critical Thinking

Thinking It Through

GLOBE FEARON
EDUCATIONAL PUBLISHER
PARAMUS, NEW JERSEY

Paramount Publishing

Executive Editor: Barbara Levadi
Editor: Carol Schneider
Editorial Assistant: Roger Weisman
Product Development: Cynthia Benjamin, Frank Puccio and Nancy Ragno
Art Director: Nancy Sharkey
Designer: Joan Jacobus
Production Director: Penny Gibson
Manufacturing Supervisor: Della Smith
Senior Production Editor: Linda Greenberg
Production Editor: Alan Dalgleish
Marketing Manager: Sandra Hutchison
Photo Research: Jenifer Hixson
Electronic Page Supervision and Production: Margarita Giammanco
Electronic Page Production: Maria Falkenberg, Joan Jacobus, José López, and Luc Van Meerbeek
Cover Design: Design Five

Globe Fearon Educational Publisher wishes to thank the following copyright owners for permission to reproduce illustrations and photographs in this book:
p. 5: Laurie Harden; **p. 7:** William Negron; **p. 21:** Joan Jacobus; **p. 23:** Steve and Mary Beran Skjold; **p. 35:** Joe Veno; **p. 36:** Beryl Goldberg; **p. 37:** Beryl Goldberg; **p. 49:** Joan Jacobus; **p. 51:** Richard Hutchings, Photo Researchers; **p. 65:** Mildred Coiro Gallo; **p. 66, 67, 68:** William Negron; **p. 69:** John Trovato; **p. 81:** William Negron; **p. 82:** Jeffrey High, Image Productions; **p. 83:** Beryl Goldberg; **p. 84:** Jeffrey High, Image Productions.

Printed in the United States of America
2 3 4 5 6 7 8 9 10 99 98 97 96 95

ISBN: 0-835-90922-0

GLOBE FEARON
EDUCATIONAL PUBLISHER
PARAMUS, NEW JERSEY

Paramount Publishing

CONTENTS

Don't Believe Everything You See and Hear 49

UNIT 5

Becoming a Smarter Consumer 65

UNIT 6

Teen Volunteers 81

Thinking about Your Future

ONE of the most important changes you'll face is the transition from school to work. You'll want to start planning for this change because, sooner or later, you'll start searching for a job. How will you go about it? What will you need to consider? How will you develop a plan of action? This unit will help you build the critical thinking skills and strategies that you'll need to answer these important questions about searching for a job.

Finding, getting, and keeping a job require critical thinking. In Lesson 1, you'll list your job goals, interests, and skills. You'll identify the kinds of jobs that are right for you. In Lesson 2, you'll predict questions an employer might ask during a job interview. In Lesson 3, you'll identify questions you have about starting a new job, and you'll learn where to find the answers to those questions.

One of the most important steps in getting a good job is to do well in the interview. As a unit project, you'll role-play with a partner. You'll act as both an interviewer and an interviewee (the person being interviewed). As the interviewee, you'll anticipate questions the interviewer (your partner) may ask. You'll also answer the questions that your partner has developed. As the interviewer, you'll develop a list of questions that you'll ask your partner.

THERE'S LIFE AFTER A JOB INTERVIEW

Shauna could hear her mother's voice inside her head: There's a difference between closing a door and slamming it. She slammed the door anyway. The sharp crack did her heart good, but the feeling didn't last very long. She was definitely late. Getting home late on Thursday was a major problem. Thursday was her night to start dinner so that her mom wouldn't have as much to do when she came home from work. Shauna checked her watch. It was already 6:15, and her mother would be home from work in half an hour. She thought about her job interview and sighed. This had been one of those days.

Wait a minute, she thought. There were terrific cooking smells coming from the kitchen. Shauna sniffed the air. Please don't let me be imagining this, she thought. Please let that really be chicken roasting in the oven just the way mom told me to do it this morning. Please let someone be doing something nice for me. She closed her eyes tight. Even if that someone is my older sister, she added to herself.

"When you weren't home by 5:30, I put the chicken in the oven. Maybe you can do something with the lettuce and tomatoes," Lucy said. "In case you forgot, most of us here on earth call it a salad." Perfect Lucy was wiping her hands on her apron. It was about three sizes too big for her. But Shauna knew this wasn't the time to make dumb apron jokes. She had tried the cute approach during her job interview. Ms. Stoner had been neither amused nor impressed.

Shauna threw her backpack on the nearest chair and followed Lucy into the kitchen. All the vegetables were lined up on the cutting board. My sister the neat freak, thought Shauna. But she meekly accepted the knife that Lucy handed her. I must be bummed, she reasoned. Even cooking dinner with my sister is looking good. As long as she doesn't ask me about the job interview this afternoon.

Lucy was setting the kitchen table. "I was thinking about you today. When's your big interview?"

Shauna started washing the vegetables, hoping that the sound of the water would drown out her answer. "Today," she mumbled. "I just got back." She was about to attack the tomatoes when she felt Lucy's disapproving eyes on her back. "You didn't wear what you have on now, did you?"

Shauna's eyes followed Lucy's. They started at her hiking boots, moved up her jeans, past her sweatshirt, and settled on her baseball cap. "Sure I did," she answered. "These are my work clothes, right? And I was applying for a job. That's work. So this is what I wore." Shauna tried to smile, but she knew Lucy wasn't buying it.

She wanted to tell her sister what happened, but she wasn't sure how to begin. Suddenly she blurted out, "The interview was a major disaster. I did everything wrong. And it wasn't just wearing the wrong clothes." Shauna was twisting her hair while she talked. The more she thought about the interview, the more she twirled her hair.

Lucy sat at the kitchen table, eating a stalk of celery. My perfect older sister, Shauna thought.

She's thin, has great skin, and eats celery instead of junk food. Unreal.

"Stop worrying," Lucy said. "I've had bad interviews. Everyone's had them. It's not the end of the world."

Shauna shook her head. "This may be the end of the world for me. I bet I never have a job in my entire life. Never."

Shauna looked at Lucy and couldn't believe her eyes. Her older sister was actually smiling. Not laughing at her. Not putting her down. She was smiling. "Hey, instead of doing a job on yourself, why don't you just tell me what happened?"

Shauna felt herself starting to relax. "I guess I didn't read the ad carefully enough. I thought they wanted a salesperson. Turns out Ms. Stoner needed a stockperson. I wasn't even sure what a stockperson does."

"It means you unpack things and put them on the shelves," Lucy said. "You would probably also help the manager with the inventory. Just the way Mom does once a month."

Shauna nodded. "That's what Ms. Stoner told me. I said it sounded fine. But I wasn't sure what 'taking inventory' meant. So I tried making a joke out of it. I said . . . Oh, forget what I said. She didn't laugh." But Lucy did. "You think it's funny? I felt like a real jerk."

"I'm sorry," Lucy answered. "But listening to you reminds me of something I did when I worked at that boutique in the mall a few summers back. I didn't understand the computer program the store used to process mail orders. It was explained in the manual, but I got so freaked that I couldn't figure out how to use it. Know what I mean?"

Shauna's hair twirling stopped. The lump in the pit of her stomach started to dissolve. Maybe, just maybe, she wasn't the only person in the world whom this had happened to. "What did you do?"

"I tried processing the orders by hand instead of using the computer. Big mistake. Finally, I asked my boss to explain the computer program to me. It took a few hours, but we finally straightened it all out."

"Didn't he fire you?" Shauna asked.

"No way," Lucy said. While she talked, she finished setting the table. "In fact, I learned something. If you don't know what to do, ask someone who does. It's the same thing with your job hunting. Next time, think about the kinds of questions the interviewer is likely to ask you. It's also helpful to find out what you can about the company and the job before the interview."

Shauna started cutting up the vegetables for dinner. But her mind was still on the interview. She knew that she was supposed to bring in two letters of recommendation from her past employers. But Mr. Garcia had moved, and she never found out his new address. She thought that one letter from the restaurant where she worked last summer would be enough. She had called the manager, Ms. Hamilton, two days ago. Was it her fault that Ms. Hamilton hadn't written the letter right away?

Suddenly, Lucy took the knife from Shauna's hand. "If you're going to slice tomatoes, slice tomatoes. . .not the kitchen sink. Why don't you tell me what else happened?"

For the first time in her life, Shauna thought that Lucy wasn't so bad . . . at least today. She decided to tell her about the rest of the interview.

"It wasn't only not knowing what a stock person does. I guess Ms. Hamilton never got around to writing me a letter of recommendation."

"When did you ask her?"

For a minute, Shauna was too absorbed in creating her special salad dressing to answer. Then she looked up at Lucy. "At least a couple of days ago. Maybe I should have given her more time?"

"Yeah! About two more weeks would have been better," Lucy answered. "When I applied for my first job at the day-care center, I didn't have the letters of recommendation Mr. Martinez asked for, either."

"But he hired you anyway, right?" Shauna asked.

Lucy set the salad bowl on the kitchen table. "Well, he gave me a job, but it wasn't the one I applied for."

Shauna added her dressing to the bowl. "Why not?"

"He wanted someone with teaching experience. I had worked at a camp for one summer. That wasn't the same thing. He ended up hiring me as a classroom assistant, not a full-time teacher."

Shauna picked up a piece of lettuce to sample her dressing. She smiled. "I guess it pays to read the job description carefully, right?"

"Absolutely. That way, you apply for a job you really can do." Lucy smiled. "It just so happened that I was offered an assistant's position. I lucked out. If I had it to do all over again, though, I'd apply only for jobs I already have the skills for."

"Thanks," Shauna said. "But there's just one problem. What will I tell Mom?"

"The truth," Lucy said. "That's what I did when I was looking for work. And she understands, believe me." Lucy nibbled at the salad and smiled. "Not bad dressing, Shauna," she said. "In fact, it's perfect. Next time you apply for a job, you might consider working as a chef."

Lesson 1: Identifying Goals, Interests, and Skills

Glancing through "Help Wanted" advertisements can be confusing. You see so many different kinds of jobs! You think: How can I find a job? Which job is the right one for me? I don't even know what I want to do or what I *can* do. Where should I begin?

The answer is, begin with yourself and not with the job. Start by discovering your own perspective, or your own viewpoint, on what you want from a job. Once you know what you want and have set goals for yourself, you'll be ready to analyze the jobs and to think critically about which job might be right for you.

One of the best ways to discover what you think about a subject is to make a cluster map. Use the cluster map below to help you identify your job goals for now and for the future. Then on a separate sheet of paper make two more cluster maps, one to focus on your interests and the other for your skills. Draw two circles to begin the clusters. In the first circle, write "What are my interests?" In the second circle, write "What skills do I have?"

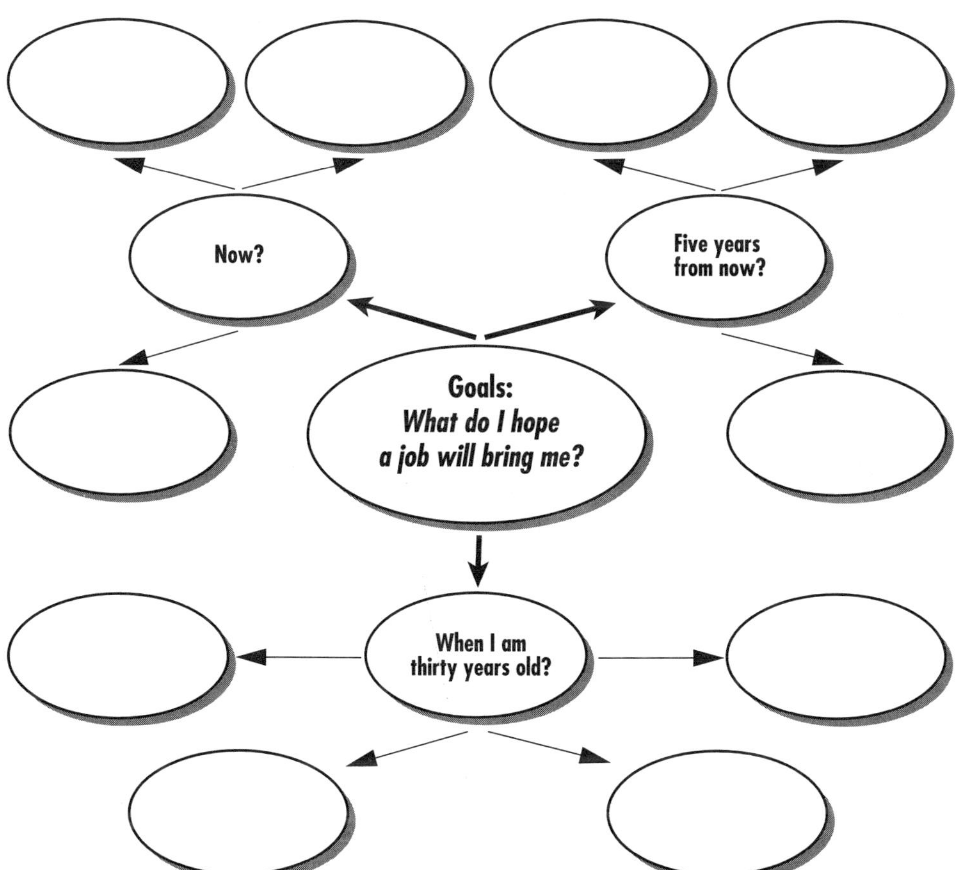

SKILLS EMPLOYERS SEEK

- ❑ analyzing
- ❑ bookkeeping
- ❑ cleaning
- ❑ computing
- ❑ cooking
- ❑ coordinating
- ❑ designing
- ❑ driving
- ❑ filing
- ❑ investigating
- ❑ keyboarding
- ❑ machine operating
- ❑ nursing
- ❑ packaging
- ❑ programming
- ❑ scheduling
- ❑ selling
- ❑ speaking
- ❑ supervising
- ❑ teaching
- ❑ translating
- ❑ typing
- ❑ writing

READING "HELP WANTED" ADS

"Help Wanted" advertisements are often written with abbreviated words. They are written this way so as to cut down on the number of words for which advertisers must pay. Most newspapers and magazines charge a fee for each word that appears in an advertisement.

The following is a key to several of the abbreviations that you'll see in classified advertisements.

- ❑ bnfts = benefits
- ❑ EOE = Equal Opportunity Employer
- ❑ exp = experience
- ❑ K = thousand
- ❑ lt = light
- ❑ M/F = male/female
- ❑ med'l = medical
- ❑ wpm = words per minute

The next step is to analyze the ideas, pick the best ones, and prioritize, or arrange them in order. Begin by making a chart. Divide a sheet of paper into three columns. Label one column "Goals," another "Interests," and the third "Skills." Using the ideas from your clusters, fill in the chart. Write each list in order of importance.

Now look at the advertisements below or bring in "Help Wanted" ads from a local newspaper that interest you. Use the three lists you just made to help you answer the questions on page 11.

BILLING

TALK TO COMPUTERS!

You'll enjoy constant communication with your computer as you use your skills in WP5.1, LOTUS, and computerized database at posh company. Excellent organizational and communication skills for challenging position. Gorgeous, comfortable working environment. Billing exp required $25K. Call Career Placement, Inc.

555-2354

INSURANCE $23K

UNDERWRITER

Excellent figure aptitude. Good communication skills a must. Some computer exp necessary. Must type 45+wpm. Full time. No fee to applicant. EOE.

CLAIMS, LTD.
Valley Creek 555-1342

LEGAL SEC'Y

ENTRY OPPORTUNITY!

Only once in a blue moon do fabulous career opptys like this come along! Major Sayville law firm will train in their own procedures and help you move UP fast! Good sec'y skills will qualify. $22K.
Call Career Placement, Inc.
555-2354

MODELS! M/F TOP $$$

International model scout featured in top mags seeks new models for designer sportswear & cosmetics. No exp necessary.

Please phone.
212-555-0707

IMMEDIATE OPENINGS

NO EXP NECESSARY

Trafalgar-based distribution center for electrical appliances is expanding to new facilities. 20 openings in 7 departments.

Company will train from ground level up. $1600/mo. while training. Neat appearance, car a must. Second language useful. Immediate hiring.

Call Monday 7-9 a.m.
555-1385

RECEPTIONIST/ CASHIER

Full-time person with pleasant personality needed for heavy phones & lt bookkeeping for auto dealer. Will train right individual. Advancement possible. Apply in person.

WARDWELL FORD
1234 Buena Vista Blvd.
Trafalgar
555-8076

SALES

JOIN AN ELITE TEAM

We are devoting every effort to developing the BEST SALES FORCE in our industry. To achieve this objective, we invest heavily in training for those who meet our rigorous qualifications.
If you are a highly motivated individual and want to take advantage of our new sales career opportunity, please call or fax resume to:

BILL O'DOUL CO.
Tel: 555-4992
Fax: 555-4968

SILK-SCREEN

OPERATOR

Rapidly growing detergent mfr has opening for a silk-screen operator. Must have good math, reading skills and ability to maintain records. Growth oppty for conscientious indiv. Excel bnfts include med'l, pension, & more. Apply in person between 4-5 p.m. EOE.

See : John Roe
Blix Chemical Co.
222 Union St.
Trafalgar

1. Which job most nearly fits your job goals? Why? ___________

2. Which job or jobs do you think would be most enjoyable, based on the interests that you have? Explain. ___________

3. In which job or jobs could you use one or more of the skills that you listed in your cluster map? Why? ___________

4. Which job or jobs could you handle right now with little or no on-the-job training? Explain. ___________

5. Which job do you think offers the best opportunities for the future? Why? ___________

SOURCES OF LEADS FOR FINDING JOBS

A survey conducted by the Bureau of the Census indicated how people find jobs. The percentage in parentheses shows how successful each method was.

- ❑ Approached employer directly (48%)
- ❑ Answered local advertisements (24%)
- ❑ Asked friends about jobs where they work (22%)
- ❑ Asked relatives about jobs where they work (19%)
- ❑ Asked friends about jobs elsewhere (12%)
- ❑ Asked relatives about jobs elsewhere (7%)

Evaluation

Use the following questions to help you evaluate your performance on this lesson.

- ❑ What did I learn about my job goals from the cluster map?
- ❑ How did making lists help me to think critically about my goals, interests, and skills?
- ❑ How did making cluster maps and lists prepare me to evaluate "Help Wanted" ads?

Lesson 2:
Predicting Interview Questions

When **predicting,** critical thinkers use what they already know. They then consider the possibilities and probabilities of what might happen in the future.

SAMPLE INTERVIEW QUESTIONS

- ❏ What is your background?
- ❏ How has your education helped to prepare you for this position?
- ❏ What previous experience have you had with this kind of work?
- ❏ What is the most important skill or quality you can bring to this company?
- ❏ What do you think is your least favorable quality?
- ❏ Why should we hire you?
- ❏ How would you describe yourself?

What do you think an employer will be looking for when he or she interviews you for a job? If you can predict what a prospective employer will ask you, you are likely to do well in the interview. One way in which you can anticipate questions that an employer will ask is to think of yourself as an employer. Imagine now that you are an employer and that you want to hire a worker for a specific position.

Because you are the boss, you make the decisions. You decide what qualities an employee should have to be effective in the position you are offering. First, decide on a name for your company and describe the position you are offering. Write this information below.

___

___

___

Next, analyze the job. Think critically about the kind of worker you should hire. Then fill in the chart below. List the qualities of your ideal job candidate.

Qualities of the Best Candidate for the Job
Appearance:
Manners/Attitude:
Work Experience:
Education:
Work Habits:
Communication Skills:
Special Skills for this Job:

Next, compile a list of questions that you, as the employer, would ask a likely employee during a job interview.

- Choose the four questions you think an employer would most likely ask and write them in the chart below. (Sample questions are listed in the side column on page 12. If you use them for ideas, write the questions in your own words.)
- Under each question, write the answer you would give if you were the one applying for the job.

Interview Questions and Answers
1. **Answer:**
2. **Answer:**
3. **Answer:**
4. **Answer:**

The following are several "sticky" situations that could arise during an interview. Discuss how you would handle each one.

- As a kid, you were a terror, the neighborhood brat. Your interviewer is a neighbor whom you used to annoy. What can you say to convince him or her that you have grown up?
- You never get above a "C," except in gym. You have had to make up some courses in summer school. If an interviewer asks you about your grades, what can you say to shift attention to your strengths?

Evaluation

Use the following questions to help you evaluate your performance on this lesson.

- ❑ How did thinking about what the employer wants help me to predict interview questions?
- ❑ Which interview questions did I answer well? Which ones were more difficult for me? Why?
- ❑ What process did I use to identify the qualities of a good job candidate?
- ❑ How can I apply this process to my own life?

Lesson 3:
Asking Questions on the Job

When you begin a job, you will have many questions about rules and procedures. Asking questions is an important part of critical thinking. In order to ask a question, you have to decide what you need to know. You have to analyze the situation and decide what information is missing.

Would you like to work in a theater? an office? a garage? an airport? a department store? Imagine your ideal working environment. Now put yourself in the picture. It is your first day on the job. You are meeting your coworkers and are getting ready to start working. What are some of the questions running through your mind? In the graphic organizer below, write the questions. A few examples are given to help you get started.

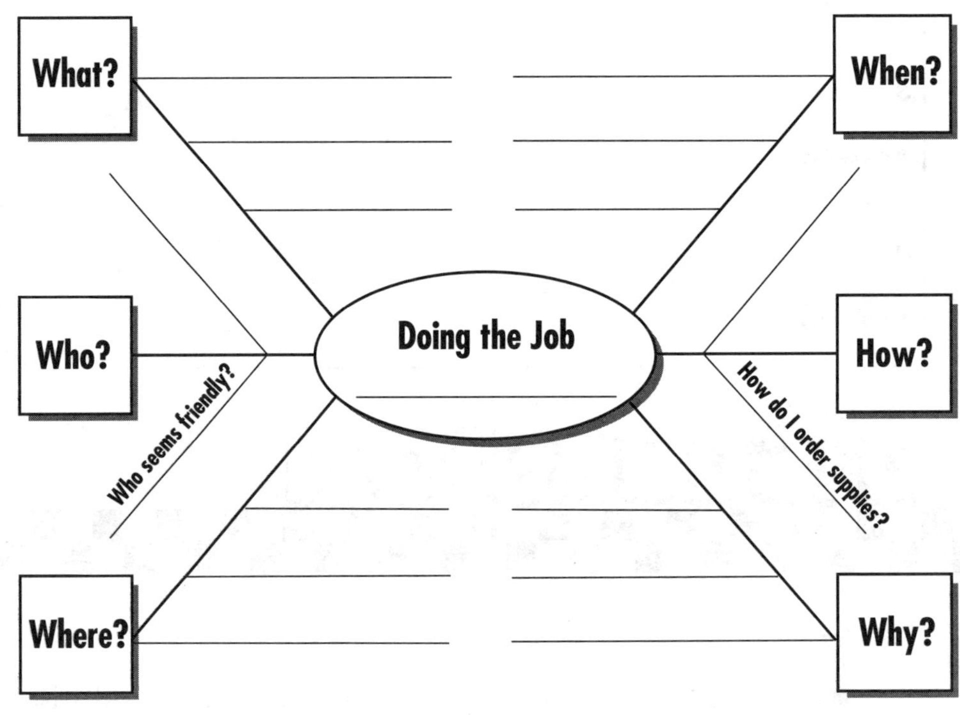

If you work for a large company, you will probably receive an employee handbook, which answers questions that employees often ask. Look at the chart on the following page. Part of a table of contents from an employee handbook appears in the left column. Read the left column carefully. Then complete the activities that follow.

BOOKSHELF

You can find many resources in a library or bookstore about job hunting and interviewing. The following are just a few of the books and videotapes. Check with your teacher, librarian, or a local bookstore owner for more titles.

Choices: A Teen Woman's Journal for Self-Awareness and Personal Planning, by Judy Edmondson and Sandy Stryker.

Interviews, Careers and the Jitterbug Blues, Beacham/Silverman Productions (videotape).

Joyce Lain Kennedy's Career Book, by Joyce Lain Kennedy and Dr. Darryl Laramore.

Summer Opportunities for Kids and Teenagers, Peterson's Guides.

The Teenage Entrepreneur's Guide: 50 Money-Making Business Ideas, by Sarah L. Riehm.

A Young Person's Guide to Getting and Keeping a Good Job, by J. Michael Farr and Marie Pavlicko.

EMPLOYEE HANDBOOK

General Facts 2

Your Working Hours; Union Membership; Vacations and Holidays; Sick Time; Employment of Relatives; Lockers; Parking; Personal Belongings; Transfers

Career Opportunities 6

Opportunities in the Company; Tuition Reimbursement; College Scholarships; In-house Credit Courses

Violations: Disciplinary Action 10

Absences from Work; Discrimination; Sexual Harassment; Offensive Conduct; Smoking; Personal Telephone Calls; Work Performance

Dismissal 15

Confidential Information; Drinking; Drugs; False Information on Employment Forms; Disrespect to Supervisors; Theft; Weapons

In the right column, write the following:

- Write three questions that would be answered in the handbook and that would likely be of great interest to you.
- Write two questions about possible difficulties you might have on the job.
- Write three questions you have that wouldn't be answered in this employee handbook.

ON THE JOB QUESTIONS

The following is a list of questions to ask yourself before you begin that important first day of work.

- ❑ Do I need to bring working papers?
- ❑ Do I have my Social Security card?
- ❑ Have I written down all the names, addresses, dates, and telephone numbers that I will need to fill out forms?
- ❑ Do I know how many deductions to claim for the income-tax form?
- ❑ Am I sure I know what time I'm expected to be on the job?

Evaluation

Use the following questions to help you evaluate your performance on this lesson.

- ❑ What did I learn about possible difficulties on the job as I thought of questions to ask?
- ❑ In what ways am I better able to meet the challenge of beginning a new job by completing this lesson?
- ❑ When I get a job, what process will I use to find out what I need to know about the company, job, and so on?

The Job Interview: A Two-Way Exchange

When you are looking for a job, sooner or later you will have a face-to-face interview with an employer. What kind of experience will this be for you? Undoubtedly, you will be nervous. From your perspective, you are "on the spot." What about the interviewer's perspective? In fact, most managers and business owners have had little training in interviewing people. Often they do not feel confident themselves about conducting job interviews. Keep in mind that your interviewer may be just as nervous as you are.

In Lesson 1, you identified job goals, interests, and skills, as well as jobs in which you are interested and for which you are well suited.

In Lesson 2, you predicted and answered interview questions.

In Lesson 3, you asked questions about a job and learned to read an employee handbook. For the unit project, you and a partner will interview each other for a job. Because a job interview is a two-way exchange of information, you'll each play both parts—that of the job applicant (or interviewee) and that of the interviewer. The unit project will help prepare you for that important event in your life: your first full-time job interview.

Identifying the Target Job...

With a partner, brainstorm the kinds of jobs that you're both interested in. List as many jobs as you can think of. Then choose one of the jobs from each of your lists by the process of elimination. As you go through each job on the list individually, evaluate whether you are truly interested in or well suited for the job. If not, cross it off. Continue this process until you only have one job listed. The job that remains will be the one that you'll be applying for when your partner interviews you.

Writing a Job Summary

Next, write a summary of your job. Keep in mind the skills and qualities the best person for the job would possess, as well as the kinds of duties that person would perform. List, for example, the job requirements that might appear in a "Help Wanted" advertisement.

Name of Job: ______________________________

Job Duties: ______________________________

____

____

____

STEP 3

Predicting Questions

Because both you and your partner will eventually play the role of the interviewee, you need to predict questions you might be asked by your partner during the interview. Working on your own, write five interview questions below that you think your partner may ask you.

1. ______________________________

____

2. ______________________________

____

3. ______________________________

____

4. ______________________________

____

5. ______________________________

____

STEP 4

Writing Questions to Ask a Job Applicant

In Step 3, you wrote questions to prepare yourself for an interview. Now you will switch your perspective to the interviewer's point of view and write questions to ask a job applicant (in this case, your partner). Give your job summary to your partner, who will use it to write interview questions to ask you.

Read your partner's job summary and ask questions about anything that you don't understand. Then use the graphic organizer below to prepare a list of questions to ask your partner. Write your questions in the boxes connected to the circle.

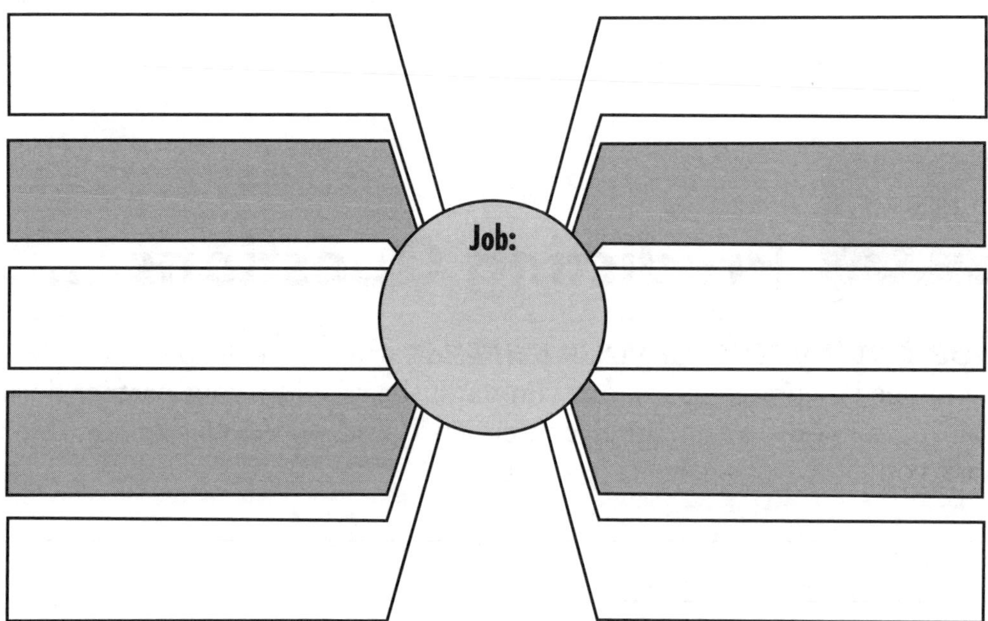

STEP 5 *Interviewing*

Next, decide which role you'll each play first. Then act out two mock job interviews to give each of you a chance to play the role of the job applicant and the interviewer. When you are the *interviewer,* begin with a question to put the applicant at ease, such as, "Did you have any trouble finding the place?" Then use the interview questions that you prepared. Be flexible, though, and ask other questions as they occur to you. End the interview with one of the following thought-provoking questions. Ask the applicant what he or she would do in one of these situations. The applicant is to take the role of a supervisor.

Case 1. Kevin is working in a bakery. One of his friends finds out that Kevin gives free doughnuts to his friends when they come in. What would you say to Kevin?

Case 2. Cheryl had to mail a thousand fliers for a sale next week. She got to the post office too late. They told her it would take two weeks to deliver the fliers at a low-cost mailing rate. As her supervisor, what would you recommend?

Case 3. Tisha's job is to answer the phone for the customer-service department of a large corporation. When she is on the phone and gets another call, the call is transferred to Bill. Bill, however, is constantly on the phone with his girlfriend, so his calls keep bouncing back to Tisha. What would you suggest that Tisha do to improve this situation?

When you are the *applicant,* or *interviewee,* listen carefully to the questions. Answer honestly and with enthusiasm. Be sure to ask questions about the job. At the end of the interview, thank the interviewer and shake hands.

If possible, tape-record or videotape your interviews so that you can play them back to see how you did. Determine which questions you answered well and which questions or answers could be improved. Practice makes perfect. If you get a chance, act out your interviews a second time, this time for the whole class.

Evaluating Your Project

Develop a set of criteria, or standards, by which you'll evaluate your project. With your partner, decide on the qualities you should have demonstrated in each role that you played. For example, you might think that an interviewer should have been able to ask questions clearly. Similarly, you might think that an interviewee should have been able to answer questions clearly. After you have developed from three to four criteria for each role, use the criteria to evaluate each other's performances in both roles.

UNIT 1 TEST

1. Circle the correct answer and explain your choice on the lines provided. An interview is important in getting a job because the employer wants to determine whether
   a. your résumé is correct.
   b. you make grammatical mistakes.
   c. you seem right for the job.
   d. you understand company policies.

Answer the following questions on the lines provided. Use examples and details to support your answers.

2. To find the right job, why does it help to think critically about your own skills and accomplishments?

3. Imagine that during an interview you are asked a question that you didn't anticipate. Describe how you would answer the question.

Answer the following essay question on a separate sheet of paper. Support your answer with examples and details.

4. Describe the steps that you will take to find a job after graduation. Include every step from start to finish, including how you will research job availability, interview for a position, and find out about the position, company, and so on.

Getting the Job You Want

YOU *never get a second chance to make a first impression.* Often an employer will get his or her first impression of you from the letter of application and résumé that you submit. You have probably noticed that most "Help Wanted" advertisements require applicants to send a letter in response to the advertisement. They may also ask for a résumé, which is a summary of your skills, educational background, and work history. In addition, if you go in person to look for a job, you may be asked to fill out an application form. From these written documents, an employer will decide whether he or she wants to interview you.

The lessons in this unit will help prepare you for the writing skills that you need to get a job and to make a good impression. In Lesson 1, you'll categorize and summarize your skills and job preferences. In Lesson 2, you'll analyze and assess your job skills in preparation for writing a résumé. In Lesson 3, you'll use critical reading skills to interpret instructions on an application form.

Finally, to pull together all the critical thinking you have done about the world of work and your place in it, you'll complete a unit project. You'll prepare a résumé, write a letter to accompany it, and fill out an application form. You'll put your critical thinking skills to work to prepare you to go out and get the job you want.

Application for Employment

Position Desired: Referred by:
Name:
Current Address:
Permanent Address:
Telephone Number:
Social Security Number:
Alien Registration Number:
Emergency Contact:
Driver's License # /State:
Education:

Work History:

Skills:

References:

Do Not Write Below this Line

Applicant's Name:
Date of Interview:

Name
Address
City, State, Zip code
Telephone number

Objective:

Skills:

Work History:

Education:

Hobbies/Interests:

References:

HOW TO LAND THE PERFECT JOB

OK, I'll give it to you straight. Looking for the perfect job is a full-time job in itself. I speak to you as one job hunter to another. We all know what hunters do, right? They plan. They stalk. They know what they want. And then they go after it. They're fearless. They're fair. They come home winners. The whole town turns out to cheer them on. I kind of like that picture, don't you? That's why I started to call myself a job hunter . . . the last of the big-time job hunters. Of course, that was before I started my first big-time job hunt.

Have you ever been on a job hunt? Sure you have. You check out the bulletin board at school or in neighborhood stores for "Help Wanted" advertisements. Then you hit the newspapers. There lots of "Help Wanted" advertisements there, right? Sure, right. But there's a catch, too. It helps to read them. When I say "read," that's exactly what I mean. Do you want to know how many times I sent out résumés in response to advertisements that read, "Two years' sales experience required." Great, I thought to myself. Didn't I sell hot dogs at our neighborhood block party for two years? Doesn't that count? Not exactly. I sent out thousands of letters telling people what a terrific salesperson I am. What happened? Nothing. Zero. Not one response.

First, let me back up a little. Maybe I didn't send out thousands of letters. Maybe it was more like hundreds. OK, so I didn't send out hundreds. I sent out twelve. Really, I did. But I learned my lesson. Rule number one: Apply for a job that's right for you. Fine, I can handle that. I look through the classified advertisements. I see that Frank's Pizza Palace needs a delivery person. I need a part-time job. Now all I have to do is write a letter explaining the kinds of jobs I've had before. It's simple. I've written letters before. I've even mailed some of them. This I'm good at.

Or am I? Have you ever tried writing a letter about your "job skills" and your "job experience"? I never have. So what? You have to start somewhere. Personally, I prefer the friendly approach. If you can toss in a couple of jokes, that's fine, too. Once I get into it, I'm really flying. I mean, this is fun. I figured I'd show it to my dad because he's been after me about this part-time job hunt for months. Did he find my letter friendly? Did he laugh at my great one-liners? Not exactly. When he handed it back, it looked like my last English paper. "Keep it organized." "Write clearly." "Explain what you mean." OK, back to the computer. A day later, I had a letter of application that even a father, or an English teacher, would love.

"But," you might ask, "did it work? Did someone from Frank's Pizza Palace answer your letter?" I'm going to keep you in suspense for a while. See, I'm not the kind of guy who waits for things to happen. I go for the gold. I climb the highest mountain. I decided to sit down and write a résumé.

You know what I'm talking about, right? You put down all the basics about yourself, like your name, address, and phone number. That part's easy. Then you list your jobs. You explain what you did and where you worked. Only this time I decided to skip the one about selling hot dogs at the block party. This is the way I looked at it. Charlie, I said to myself—I don't like calling myself Charles when I talk to myself—it pays to be prepared. My sister, who's been working like forever, said that it's important to have a résumé. It explains my "job history." So I ask her what I should do with this great résumé of mine. "Simple," she says. "When you write a letter of application, put your résumé in the same envelope." Now she tells me!

OK, so I mail it the day after. And I wait and wait and . . . Hey, wait a minute. What do I find in the mail three weeks later? Is it a letter from Frank's Pizza Palace offering me a job? Not exactly. It's a letter from old Frank telling me I have to fill out an application for the job. I told you this job hunting can get complicated. But nothing's going to stop me now. I read the instructions on the application. They make sense. It's a lot like writing your résumé. You know, the basics: name, address, education, work history. My father tells me to play it straight. There's something else, too. Be honest. Sure, I wanted to say I had managed a restaurant several years ago, when I was in the eighth grade. But I'm not playing that game. So I fill in all the blanks . . . and I mean every single one. I even typed it, since my mother told me that she hasn't been able to read a single card I've sent her since I started putting stamps on envelopes.

Now we're getting to the good part. I can see that you're waiting to find out what happened . . . like, did he or didn't he? Well, you can relax. Sure, it didn't happen right away. As my dad always says, "Good things generally take some time." That's a little wisdom I decided to throw in here. There's a serious side to me, too. I mean, working at Frank's Pizza Palace is serious work. People depend on me. But you know something? It's fun, too. I kind of like having a job. I like the paycheck, too. As my dad says, "If you try hard enough, you'll find a job in the end." And you know something? He's right.

Lesson 1: Categorizing Job Skills and Preferences

CATEGORIES OF JOBS

- **Professional:** engineer, architect, scientist, lawyer, teacher, librarian, doctor, reporter, writer, actor, musician
- **Technicians:** laboratory technician, optician, nurse, pilot, air-traffic controller
- **Sales:** insurance agent, real estate agent, travel agent
- **Administrative Support:** bank teller, office clerk, secretary, court reporter, word processor
- **Service:** corrections officer, firefighter, guard, detective, chef, dental assistant, flight attendant, mechanic
- **Construction:** bricklayer, carpenter, carpet installer, roofer, electrician, tile setter
- **Production:** assembler, factory supervisor, butcher, meat inspector, jeweler, textile worker, toolmaker
- **Transportation:** bus driver, pilot, railroad engineer, ship captain, taxi driver

When you write for a job, you tell your prospective employer about the skills and abilities you'll bring to the job. Before you can tell an employer these things, however, you have to identify what they are. When you first enter the work force, you have not yet had a chance to find out what you can really do. How can you know what your skills are? First, you have to examine your interests. Your interests are a key to your skills, because people usually like to do the things they do well.

In the list below, circle every item that names something you like to do. Be honest with yourself. If you don't especially enjoy something, don't circle it.

I like to

Be a leader	Decorate	Figure out how things work	Take things apart
Be a part of a team	Read	Solve problems	Be in charge
Work on crafts	Write	Take photographs	Keep accurate records
Fix things	Figure out how things work	Organize information	Sell a product or an idea
Sing	Give advice	Speak in public	Operate equipment
Play a musical instrument	Do research	Work with my hands	Meet the public
Influence others	Dance	Create	Compete
Entertain others	Act	Learn something new	Cooperate
Make videos or movies	Drive	Negotiate	Organize people
Set up machinery	Work on art	Teach or train others	Work with numbers
Serve others	Help those in trouble	Contruct things	Program computers
Make decisions	Talk	Listen	Organize projects

What else do you like to do that isn't listed? ____________________

____

Next, categorize your skills. Go back to the items you circled in the previous chart. On the following chart, write each item in the column in which it belongs. For example, if you circled "Be a leader," you would write it in the column labeled "Working with People." (Some items could be listed in more than one column.)

Working with People	Working with Things
Working with Ideas	**Working with the Arts**

Next, read over your four lists. In each column, put a check mark next to the three things that you like to do best.

1. What conclusions can you draw from the graphic organizer? What does it tell you about what you like to do? ____________________

____

2. Why is it important to know your skills and interests when you look for a job? ____

____

You've heard the saying a thousand times: *Honesty is always the best policy.* Yet, when it comes to developing a résumé, some people are tempted to exaggerate their skills and job history.

Imagine that a friend was making false claims on his or her résumé, what would you tell your friend? Are employers likely to verify information on an applicant's résumé? What are the consequences of falsifying information?

To categorize means to classify or to put into categories. In this case, you are grouping skills and interests that apply to different work categories.

Evaluation

Use the following questions to help you evaluate your performance on this lesson.

- ❏ Which items were hardest for me to categorize? Why?
- ❏ What did I learn about myself after completing this lesson that I didn't realize before?

Lesson 2:
Analyzing and Assessing Job Skills

When you apply for a full-time job, most employers ask to see a résumé. Even if they don't ask you for one, having a résumé gives you an advantage over other job candidates and helps you to know what to say in a job interview. To write a résumé, you need to ask yourself two questions: *What job am I seeking?* and *What skills will I bring to the job?*

The first question should be easy to answer if you are responding to a "Help Wanted" advertisement, since the job title is usually given in the advertisement. For example, the advertisement might say, "Secretary for Advertising Agency" or "Security Guard." If you are not applying for a specific job, you may write a more general description, such as "Entry-level position in advertising." Think of a job you want and write its title and description below. Then write a statement telling the kind of job you are looking for, which is called a Job Objective.

Job Description: ____

____

____

____

Job Objective: ____

____

____

The second question requires critical thinking. You need to think about your skills, compare them with the skills required for the job, and then decide which skills will transfer to the job.

To see how this works, read the example in the sidenote. Then think of similar examples from your own life. What work have you done? What have you learned? Think about part-time jobs, volunteer work, and extra-curricular activities. Don't forget your helping with chores at home, running errands for your grandmother, baby-sitting, delivering newspapers, selling candy door-to-door, working at a school fair, decorating the gym for a dance. Think about your courses in school and other ways in which you have acquired skills. Let your mind run free. Write your ideas in the chart on the next page.

SKILLS THAT TRANSFER TO A JOB

Kima is applying for a job as a bank teller. What skills can she transfer to that job? She knows something about the business because she has a savings account and checking account and knows how they work. She took *math courses* in school. She knows how to use a *calculator* and an *adding machine*. She also took Business English, which helped her develop *business communication skills*. During the summer, she sold food at a refreshment stand. Her employer trusted her to *handle money*, *supervise* younger employees, and *deal with the public*. She was *punctual*, never late to work. She was *seldom absent*. She was *dependable* and *hard working*. Her employer told her that she had a *good attitude*. Kima was also given *responsibility* as a baby-sitter. In that job, she showed *initiative* and *good judgment* in *dealing with children* and in *helping them settle arguments* that frequently arose. In short, Kima has developed many skills to offer an employer.

JOB OR LEARNING EXPERIENCE	SKILLS I USED

Now look over your notes on the chart. Circle the skills that you could use on the job you want.

The skills you chose are the details that you will use to convince an employer to interview you for a job. The main idea you want to convey is that you have the skills to do the job. On the lines below, write a statement to an employer in which you state why you are a strong candidate for the job you want most.

____

____

____

____

____

____

____

DISCUSSION

Some people spend more time planning how they will spend their weekend than how they will spend the rest of their lives. How does this statement apply to looking for a job? What might happen if you don't look to the future when you think about getting a job? How do people end up getting stuck in dead-end jobs that they don't even like?

BOOKSHELF

You can find many resources in a library or bookstore about applying for a job. The following are just a few of the books that are available. Check with your teacher, librarian, or a local bookstore owner for more titles.

American Almanac of Jobs and Salaries, by John Wright.

The Young Learner's Handbook: A Guide to Solving Problems, Mastering Skills, Thinking Creatively, by Stephen Tchudi.

Evaluation

Use the following questions to help you evaluate your performance on this lesson.

- ❑ What process did I use to choose my skills?
- ❑ Did I think of any job skills that I wish I had or skills that I would like to improve? If so, which ones? If not, why not?
- ❑ Was I surprised by any of my findings when I listed my skills? Explain.

Lesson 3:
Interpreting Instructions on an Application Form

Chances are you will have to fill out an application form to get a job. If you walk into a company and ask for a job, you will probably be handed an application form to fill out before you will be considered for a position. Even if you send a résumé, you will still be asked to fill out an application form.

Application forms make it easy for an employer to compare candidates because all the forms are the same. To find out about candidates' previous work experience, for example, an employer knows just where to look on the application.

Because application forms make it easy to compare job candidates, they are also used to eliminate candidates. That's why you must read every item carefully and think before you write. Some application forms have tricky instructions designed to see how well you follow directions. The following are several examples of mistakes that you can make if you are not a critical reader.

INSTRUCTION ON FORM	MISTAKES OFTEN MADE
Write in blue or black ink.	Write in pencil.
Position Applied For:	Skip this, since you don't know the answer.
Name: Last, First, Middle	Write your first name first. If you have no middle name, don't write one.
Check the business machines you know how to use.	Circle the machines you can use.
Do not write below this line.	Fill in the blanks below the line.
Current address:	Skip it, since you have listed your permanent address.
Fill in your Employment History below.	Write, "See attached résumé."
Why did you leave your previous job?	Write "I was fired."

HINTS FOR APPLICATION FORMS

Check spelling. Carry a pocket dictionary with you.

Do not leave any blanks. If an item does not apply to you, write NA (*not applicable*).

Choose your words carefully. Not, "I was fired," but "I was dismissed," or "terminated by mutual agreement."

Some questions are illegal. You do not have to fill in information about your race, religion, or marital status.

Referred by. How you found out about the job.

Emergency Contact. The person to call if something happens to you on the job.

Permanent Address. Your home address.

Current Address. Where you are currently living. Write "Same" if you are living at the permanent address.

Alien Registration Number. A number you are issued if you are not a United States citizen.

References. People who would be willing to give you a good recommendation.

Read the "Hints for Application Forms" sidenotes on page 28. Then fill in the application form.

Please Print in Ink

Position Desired: ____________________

Referred by: ____________________

Name: (First, Middle, Last) ____________________

Telephone: ____________________

Emergency Contact: ____________________

Telephone: ____________________

Permanent Address: ____________________

Current Address: ____________________

Social Security #: ____________________

Alien Registration #: ____________________

EDUCATION: SUMMARIZE YOUR EDUCATION BELOW. INCLUDE THE DATE YOU GRADUATED OR YOUR EXPECTED GRADUATION DATE.

Which languages other than English do you speak? ____________________

Check machines you operate: Typewriter, Computer, Calculator, Adding Machine, Dictaphone

WORK: SUMMARIZE YOUR WORK EXPERIENCE. STATE: (1) DATES YOU WORKED; (2)EMPLOYER; (3) RESPONSIBILITIES; (4) REASON FOR LEAVING.

Have you ever been convicted of a felony? ____________________

References: ____________________

- -

Do Not Write Below This Line

Applicant's Name :____________________

Date of Interview: ____________________

Interpreting means to give your own thoughts and ideas about something and place it in the context of your own experience, perspective, and point of view. Critical thinkers are able to tell their interpretations from evidence or fact.

Evaluation

Use the following questions to help you evaluate your performance on this lesson.

- ❑ Which items on the application form gave me the most difficulty? Why?
- ❑ Is my application filled out neatly? What impression will it give an employer? Explain.
- ❑ Did I accurately follow all directions on the application form? If not, why not?

Applying for a Job

Applying for a job takes planning, preparation, and thinking. Once you lay the groundwork, however, you are ready to take that next big step: applying for a job in writing. In this project, you will learn how to do this. You will write a résumé and a letter of application. You will also write and fill out an application form.

STEP 1 Writing a Résumé...............

A résumé summarizes your educational background, skills, accomplishments, and work history. Its purpose is to convince an employer to interview you for a job. Read the "Help Wanted" advertisements in your city or local newspaper. Select a job that you are interested in and one that you feel you are well suited for. Write your job choice below.

My Job Choice: ____

Based on the "Help Wanted" advertisement or your knowledge of the job, list four skills that you should emphasize on your résumé.

1.____

2.____

3.____

4.____

A résumé should fit on one side of an $8^{1}/_{2}$–by–11 inch sheet of paper. You can design it yourself, using the diagram below as a model. Don't use all the headings shown. Select only the ones you think need to be included. Cross out the others. Write a first draft of your résumé. Then edit the first draft and proofread it for errors. Type your final draft or have someone type it for you.

[Name]
[Street Address]
[City, State, ZIP] [Telephone Number]

Job Objective

Education

Work Experience
(include most recent job and earlier job(s))

Skills

Accomplishments

Interests

Community Service

Hobbies

Personal Data

STEP 2

Writing a Cover Letter

When you send out your résumé, you will need to include a cover letter, also called a letter of application. A cover letter is short and to the point. Its purpose is to attract an employer to read your résumé and to interview you. Use the sample on page 32 to write a cover letter for your résumé.

Your Street
City, State ZIP
Date

Name of Employer and Job Title
Company Name
Company Address
City, State ZIP

Dear ________:

Paragraph 1: State why you are writing. Are you answering a Help Wanted ad? responding to the advice of a friend or relative? writing because you have always wanted to work for that company?

Paragraph 2: Explain how you meet the qualifications listed in the ad or why you are qualified to do the job.

Paragraph 3: Say that your résumé is enclosed and request an interview.

Sincerely yours,
(Your Signature)
Your Name
Your Telephone Number

Creating an Application Form.........

Imagine yourself in a Human Resources office. You, along with a dozen other applicants, are filling out application forms. But you have an advantage. You take out an application form that you have developed and simply copy the information requested. Having the information you need at your fingertips is a great advantage.

Working in a small group, brainstorm the items to include in an application form. One person in the group can be the recorder and jot down your ideas. You may wish to use these major categories:

Personal Data

Education

Experience and Skills

References

After brainstorming, discuss all the choices and eliminate the items that you feel are unnecessary. Then create a sample application form. (Don't fill in any of the blanks.) Exchange your form with another group. Read that group's form and determine whether you understand all the directions on the form. Discuss with that group anything that you think is unclear.

With your own group, revise your application form, based on the feedback you received. Copy your group's application form and fill in each item. You're all set. You have an application form that you can use to guide you in your next job search.

Publishing and Evaluating

As a class, make a loose-leaf book labeled *Help Wanted*, which students may use as a reference for job hunting. Each person should contribute a résumé, cover letter, or application form. As a group, decide which items you will contribute to the class book.

If you want a job right now, you probably have been preparing materials with an eye toward applying for a particular job. If so, you are well prepared. You are ready to send out your cover letter and résumé—and get that job!

1. Circle the correct answers and explain your choices on the lines provided.
A cover letter shows your ability to
a. tell about your hobbies.
b. give your job history.
c. interest an employer in reading your résumé.
d. explain your résumé to an employer.

2. The importance of a résumé is that it
a. tells your job history.
b. replaces an interview.
c. tells your race and religion.
d. introduces you to a possible employer.

Answer the following questions on the lines provided. Use examples and details to support your answers.

3. A résumé usually does not contain much personal information about you. What do you think should be your main consideration in deciding what personal information to include in your résumé?

? Answer the following essay question on a separate sheet of paper. Support your answer with examples and details.

4. Your company has placed a "Help Wanted" advertisement in a local newspaper. Your boss asks you to go over the 300 résumés that came in from people seeking the job. She wants you to cut the number of applicants down to the 10 who will be interviewed. How will you go about eliminating candidates? Describe both the process and the standards you will use to eliminate 290 résumés.

Thinking about Living Independently

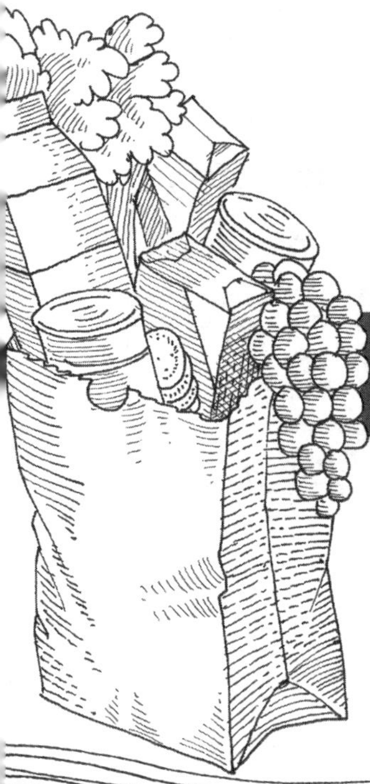

HAVE you ever spent time away from home without any older adults around? What does it feel like to be on your own?

Even if you live at home, as you get older you become and more independent. You think about your future and how you can shape it. With this life change comes more responsibility. You make more decisions, many of which affect your future. Being independent calls for you to make good decisions.

In this unit, you'll think critically about living independently.You'll think about your future and set some long-term and short-term goals for yourself. You'll gather information about living independently. You'll learn to use criteria for evaluating information in order to make objective decisions. You'll also prioritize alternatives for good decision making.

For the unit project, you'll analyze and evaluate decisions that you make at home, in school, and at your job. Then you'll use that information to set goals and to develop a plan for reaching those goals.

I Want to Be Me!

This week's edition of *Young Living* takes a closer look at an ever-increasing trend among young people: living independently. Today, more and more young adults are giving up the security of living at home and are making a life of their own. In this article, *Young Living* talks to a few of these young adventurers and their parents.

Meet Aaron. Aaron is nineteen years old and lives on his own. He holds a full-time job as a receptionist at a major corporation. Aaron attends evening classes at the local community college and is studying to be a financial planner. Financial planners suggest ways in which individuals can invest their money. In response to *Young Living*'s question about what Aaron likes about living independently, Aaron replied, "This is the greatest experience of my life. I have opportunities to do things and to meet people that I would not have if I were living at home. Money is a lot tighter, but I'm learning to stay on a budget and to live within my means."

Young Living also asked Aaron to talk about his most humorous independent-living experience. He chuckled a bit and told us this story. "I was moving into my third-floor apartment. My friends were helping me carry a couch up three flights of stairs. We were halfway up the third flight when we lost control of the couch. It slid down the stairs and through the front door of apartment 2A. Luckily, no one was injured. What a way to get to meet your neighbors, and it cost me three hundred dollars to boot!"

Now meet Jennifer. Jennifer is moving back home after living independently for almost eight months. When asked why she moved back home, this is what Jennifer said. "I just couldn't seem to make ends meet. I had too much month left at the end of my money. Then my hours at my job were cut back from 40 to 25 hours per week. I just couldn't make it, so I asked Mom if I could come back home. Thank goodness she welcomed me with open arms, or I might be living on the street."

Jennifer offered this advice to other young adults who are thinking of living independently. "First, make sure you have at least two month's rent saved in your bank account and don't touch that money no matter what happens. Second, be disciplined. No one is telling you what to do or when to do it. So, if you don't get things done, no one will be there to do them for you. Third, be neat. Set some time aside to clean your apartment and to do your laundry. Mom isn't following you around anymore."

Finally, *Young Living* discussed independent living with Aaron's and Jennifer's parents. Aaron's parents were hesitant at first about letting their son move out on his own. They didn't think he was mature enough to handle all of the responsibilities. They are very happy that things have worked out for Aaron.

Jennifer's mom felt that moving out was a good idea. It was a chance for Jennifer to mature and to learn about life. She had no problems taking Jennifer back home. She preferred that Jennifer try and fail than never try at all. Her mother already has noticed a greater maturity in Jennifer than was there before Jennifer left home.

So there you have it. Two different young people experiencing independent living with two different results. Think about those experiences and how they can help you decide whether you are ready to live independently. To make this decision, you must think about such things as rent money, food money, and car and insurance payments. Don't forget to keep some money for recreation. Then talk to other teens or young adults, your parents, and teachers, who are living on their own or who have had more life experiences than you have had. Listen to what they have to say. If you prepare yourself by doing these things, your experiences with independent living may be much more pleasurable and rewarding.

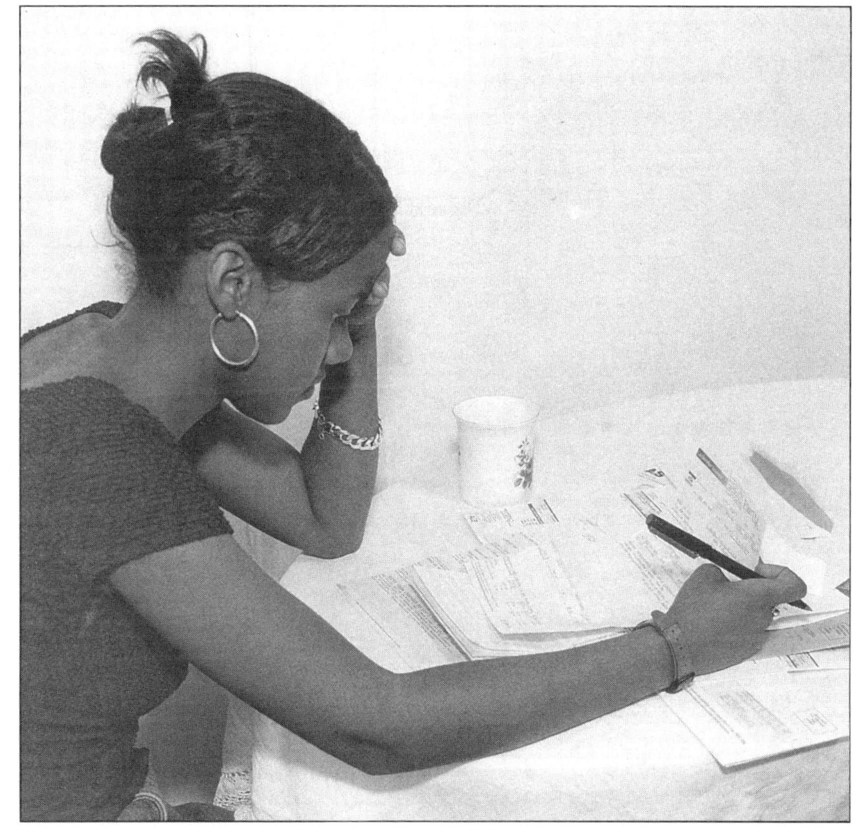

Lesson 1:
Setting Goals for the Future

THE LANGUAGE OF THINKING

Setting goals requires thinking and planning. To set long-term goals, for example, you need to identify the goals first. Then you need to break each goal into smaller goals, or steps. As you complete each step, you are moving toward your end goal. You can easily monitor your progress toward your end goal as you reach each smaller goal.

Have you ever thought about what you will be doing next week? next month? How about next year, or ten years from now? When looking into your future, it's important to have goals—both short-term and long-term goals. Short-term goals are ones that can be achieved in a relatively short period of time; long-term goals are ones that take a long period of time to achieve. For example, a short-term goal is to do well on your math final exam at the end of the school year. An example of a long-term goal is to be the first person in your family to earn a college degree.

Use the following graphic organizer to list two short-term and two long-term goals. Once you have identified your goals, answer the questions on page 39 to help you establish plans to achieve each goal. Then complete the graphic organizer.

Goal:

Plan:

Goal:

Plan:

Long-Term Goals

My Personal Goals

Short-Term Goals

Goal:

Plan:

Goal:

Plan:

PERSONAL GOALS

Set goals that

- ❑ challenge you
- ❑ are realistic and attainable
- ❑ make use of your talents and interests
- ❑ are measurable

1. What are my personal interests? ______________________________

____

2. How do I define personal success? ____________________________

____

3. What are some goals that I have already accomplished? __________

____

4. What skills do I need to achieve my goals? ____________________

____

____

5. How can I break long-term goals into a series of short-term goals? Select one long-term goal from the graphic organizer on page 38. Use the lines below to sequence steps, or smaller goals, that will lead you to your long-term goal. ______________________

____

____

____

____

____

6. How will I know when I have achieved my goals? ______________

____

____

____

DISCUSSION

Sometimes the goals that we set for ourselves do not meet expectations that others have of us. What are some ways to resolve these differences in expectations? What can you learn from experienced adults when setting your goals? How much should you rely on your own feelings and wishes when setting your goals?

HOW TO WRITE A GOAL

Goals should be written using the following formula:

Action verb + task + measurement

Using action verbs helps you and others to identify what you will do to achieve your goal. The task is the goal itself. The measurement can be either a statement that describes how you will measure or determine when you have reached your goal or one that tells the date by which you will have reached your goal. The following are examples of long-term goals:

- ❑ I will live on my own by the time I am 25 years old.
- ❑ I will save $2,000 for living expenses by the end of the year.

Evaluation

Use the following questions to help you evaluate your performance on this lesson.

- ❑ What process did I use to establish my goals?
- ❑ What personal experiences did I draw upon to identify my goals?
- ❑ What did I find difficult when identifying my goals? How did I overcome these difficulties?

Lesson 2:
Evaluating Information

Along the way toward your goals, you will make a lot of choices and decisions. To make any well-informed choice, you need good information. Information is power. The more information you have, the better your decisions will be. You may rarely feel that you have all the information you would like to have to make an important decision. However, you can do a few things to be sure the information you get is useful and reliable.

1. **Know what you want.**
   Clarify your goals so that you can collect useful information.

2. **Consider the source.**
   Does the person providing the information want to tell only one side of the story?

3. **Listen to information that you don't want to hear.**
   To make an informed decision, you should consider all of the available information. Be aware when you are making decisions based on emotions, not facts.

4. **Consult several sources.**
   If you find conflicting information, look for more sources to verify your facts.

Imagine that you're trying to decide between two jobs. List the sources you will use to help you make your decision. Remember to consider your long-term and short-term goals, as you did in Lesson 1.

______________________ ______________________

______________________ ______________________

______________________ ______________________

Think of a place away from your home where you would like to spend the next year of your life. Don't worry about the cost or

THE LANGUAGE OF THINKING

To evaluate is to judge or to determine the worth or value of something. Whenever you form an opinion, you are making an evaluation. Insofar as possible, your opinions should be based, not on emotions, but on reason, evidence, logic, and good sense.

When you evaluate information to make good decisions, ask yourself questions such as the following:

- ❑ Is this information relevant to my decision? In other words, does it get at the point of the decision?
- ❑ Is my source objective, or am I just getting one side of a story?
- ❑ Am I being objective and unemotional about this decision? Am I hearing information that I don't want to hear?
- ❑ To get a balanced view, have I consulted more than one expert?

any obligations that you may have at this point. For now, decide where you would like to live independently for a year. Then answer the following questions.

1. What places (alternatives) can you immediately think of where you would like to live for the next 365 days? List them.

______________________ ______________________

______________________ ______________________

2. How much do you know about each of the alternatives that you listed? Rate each one: **2** = know a lot about it, **1** = know a little about it, **0** = know nothing specific about it,-**1** = know nothing but would just like to go there.

______________________ ______________________

______________________ ______________________

3. Classify your sources of information about each alternative that you ranked as 2 or 1. Label the information about each place as **E** = your own experience, if you've been there; **H** = heard about it from people whose judgment you respect; **R** = read information about the place.

______________________ ______________________

______________________ ______________________

4. Which label appeared most often? ______________________

How certain are you about the value of the information that you have? ______________________

5. If you had to choose a place to go, what additional information do you think you'd need? Why? ______________________

____

6. What sources would you explore for this information?

____

7. What role do you think your own experience should play in gathering information? Why? ______________________

____

BOOKSHELF

You can find many resources in a library or bookstore about living independently. The following are just a few of the books that are available. Check with your teacher, librarian, or a local bookstore owner for more titles.

Living on Your Own, by Greta Walker.

Money of Your Own, by Grace W. Weinstein.

Smart Choices, by Nancy Kolodny, Robert Kolodny, and Thomas Bratter.

Go For It: Get Organized, by Sara Gilbert.

Evaluation

Use the following questions to help you evaluate your performance on this lesson.

- ❏ What process did I use to evaluate information?
- ❏ How can I gather information more effectively in order to make informed decisions?
- ❏ How can I use what I have learned in this lesson in making decisions about my personal life?

Lesson 3:
Prioritizing Alternatives

Every day you face situations in which you have to make decisions. These situations may be at home, in school, or on your job. Most people have little practice in decision-making skills, yet everyone is expected to make decisions throughout life. Read the "Facts about Decisions" in the sidenote on page 43. Discuss these "facts" in a small group.

Describe a critical decision that you're facing. Your decision could come from questions, such as: What should I do after high school? What should I do about my girlfriend/boyfriend? What can I do to earn money? How can I make my life happier?

____

____

____

Now try to think of several actions and decisions that you might make in this situation. List at least four of them, including ones that you may not like at this time.

Alternative 1 ________________________________

Alternative 2 ________________________________

Alternative 3 ________________________________

Alternative 4 ________________________________

It is impossible to make good decisions if you aren't clear about what is important to you in a given situation. One powerful influence in decisions is your values: the things that you think are important. The following are eight common values.

honesty	______	*friends*	______
independence	______	*satisfaction*	______
money	______	*prestige*	______
security	______	*free time*	______

In the space next to each value, write a number from 1 to 8, to show how you would rank, or prioritize, that value. For example, if friends are the most important to you, assign it a 1. If free time is the least important, assign it an 8.

THE LANGUAGE OF THINKING

To **prioritize** means to rank, or to put in order of importance. You put the most important thing first, the next important thing second, and so on.

We prioritize in many areas of our lives. For example, have you ever had too many things to do in one day, and you knew that you would never get them all done? You had to decide which activities absolutely needed to be done first and which could wait. When you did that, you were prioritizing.

In order to prioritize actions, you need to use several criteria. Usually you would ask yourself what values you have that this action will appeal to. Then, based on the values that are most important to you in this situation, you could choose the alternative that is best for you.

For each of the alternative actions or decisions you wrote, think about the values that it might indicate. For example, if your decision involves the kind of job that you should take for the summer, it might indicate that you value money or prestige. Another decision might show that you value honesty or job satisfaction. On the following chart, write your decision and your four alternatives for it. Write all the values that each alternative might indicate. Include the priority ranking number you assigned for each value.

DECISION	
Alternative 1: **Values:**	**Alternative 2:** **Values:**
Alternative 3: **Values:**	**Alternative 4:** **Values:**

Now look at the results and answer the following questions:

1. Which alternative accommodated the greatest number of values?

____

2. Which alternative accommodated the most important values, according to your ranking? _______________________

____

3. Which alternative do you think is the best choice? Why? ______

____

____

4. Did you learn anything new about yourself? Explain. ________

____

____

5. Perhaps there are more alternatives that you haven't thought about. Where might you get information to increase your options?

____

FACTS ABOUT DECISIONS

There are several important things you should know about decision making:

- ❑ A decision is the act of choosing among several possibilities.
- ❑ An outcome is the result or consequence of a person's action or decision.
- ❑ A good decision is one in which the person chooses the alternative that is best, according to his or her preferences, needs, or values.

Evaluation

Use the following questions to help you evaluate your performance on this lesson.

- ❑ What process did I use to prioritize alternative actions?
- ❑ What values are the most important to me? What other values would I add to the eight in the lesson?
- ❑ What has this lesson taught me about the challenge of being an independent thinker and a responsible person?

Preparing for Life's Decisions

How prepared are you to make important decisions about your life? It's not as easy to make the correct choices as you might think. You can prepare yourself now by doing three things. First, look at where you are. Then decide where you want to go. Finally, determine how to get there.

The three lessons in this unit have already started this process. In Lesson 1, you set some long-term and short-term goals. In Lesson 2, you learned about analyzing sources of information. In Lesson 3, you prioritized alternative actions for decision making.

For the unit project, you'll apply what you learned in these lessons to your personal life. Think about the opportunities that are available to you at home, in school, and at work to help you on your way to future success.

STEP 1 Computing Your Time Each Day

In a small group, discuss the amount of time that each of you spends doing things related to your home, school, and job. Record an approximate total number of hours devoted each day to these three categories. Obviously, the total cannot exceed 24 hours. Create a pie chart similar to the one below, showing the percentage of time your group spends each day on home-, school-, and work-related activities.

To determine an average number of hours per day, add up the total hours in each category. Then divide by the number of people in your group. To get a percentage, divide that hourly average by 24. For example, let's say there are three people in your group. Student A spends 8 hours doing school-related activities, Student B spends 9 hours, and Student C spends 7 hours. The average number of hours would be 8. The following shows you how to find the average:

Our Average Day

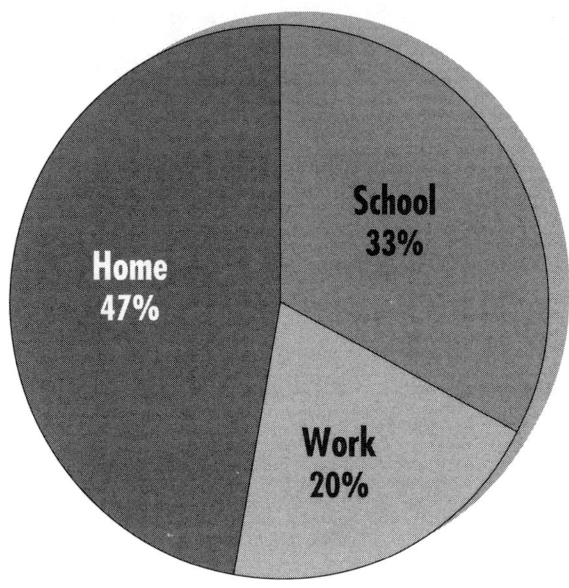

8 + 9 + 7 = 24

24 ÷ 3 = 8 hours

8 hours ÷ 24 hours = .33, or 33 percent

The percentage of their 24-hour day spent on school-related activities is 33 percent.

STEP 2

Setting Goals

Next, you need to identify your long-term goals. Individually, complete the diagram below with your long-term goals. In each of the outside circles, list your long-term goals for each of the following categories: home, school, work. There is no right or wrong number of responses. Add or subtract circles from your diagram as necessary.

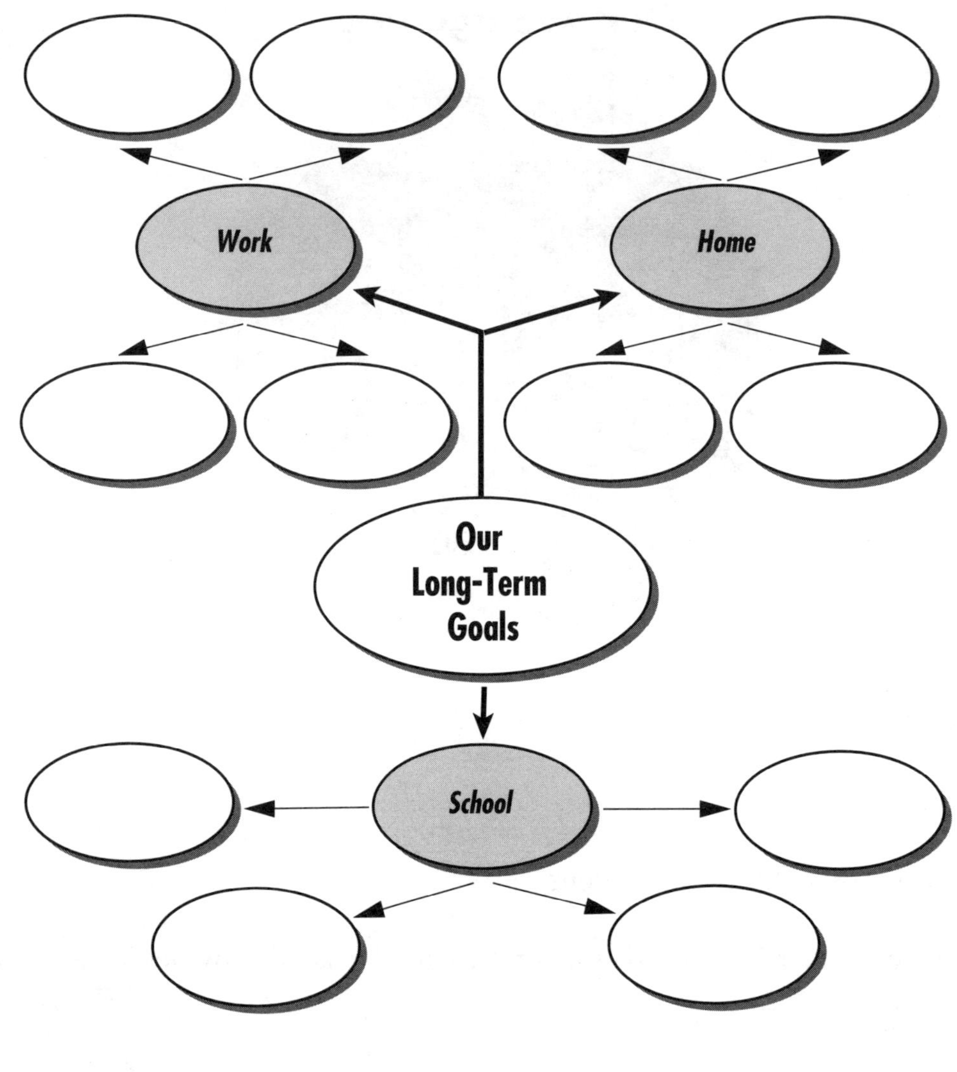

Making a Plan

Now that each of you knows where you are and where you would like to go, you need to come up with a plan for getting there. Individually, write or type a statement explaining how you plan to achieve your goals. The statements should be divided into the same three categories: home, school, and work. They should include a description of how you plan to make decisions and gather good information. Remember the following steps:

1. Know what you want. Clarifying your goals will help you gather important information.

2. Consider your sources of information. Are they reliable?

3. Listen to information that you may not want to hear. Try to be objective.

4. If possible, consult more than one source of information.

Conclude this step by sharing your plan with your group.

Evaluating the Project

Evaluate your work on this project by answering the questions below.

1. How did this project help me to learn about the personal decisions that I have to make?

2. Which part of the project did I have the most difficult time completing? Why?

3. How did this project help me to set personal goals?

4. Which critical thinking skills did I use during this project? How did I practice these skills?

UNIT 3 TEST

1. Circle the correct answers and explain your choices on the lines provided.
   When setting goals, it is important to
   a. make goals that are easily attainable.
   b. constantly change your goals.
   c. set goals that are realistic.
   d. keep your goals private

2. Put an X next to the statement that is true and explain your choice.
   ❒ Many people avoid decisions because they don't have enough information.
   ❒ Personal experience has no important role in decision making.

Answer the following questions on the lines provided. Use details and examples to support your answers.

3. In what ways will thinking about long-term and short-term goals prepare you for living independently?

? **Answer the following essay question on a separate piece of paper. Support your answer with examples and details.**

4. Why are a person's values important in prioritizing and choosing among alternative actions?

UNIT 4

DOWNSIZING
RIGHTSIZING
PINK-SLIPPED
(Firing)

Don't Believe Everything You See and Hear

WORDS are powerful—and like many other kinds of power, their use can be abused. Words can influence your decisions and your actions. They can affect what you buy, what you wear, what you eat, how you act, and what you do—or don't do. They can affect ideas you support or oppose, and they can also change the way you see, or perceive, things.

The misuse of language is an important issue, especially in a democracy. A democracy needs citizens who recognize language misuse when they meet it. A democracy needs citizens who think critically and who don't believe everything that they see and hear.

In this unit, you'll identify common abuses of language. You'll distinguish between fact and opinion. You'll compare meanings of synonyms to discover how words are chosen to influence your feelings. You'll also examine sexist language and other stereotypes and will judge how they are abuses of language.

As a unit project, you'll find examples of misuse of language in the media. You'll analyze how the writer has used language in an attempt to trick the audience. You'll rewrite several examples in "honest" language. Then you'll share the original and your revised versions with the class.

HAIR IMPAIRED
(Bald or Balding)

VERTICALLY CHALLENGED
(Short)

MISSPOKE
(LIED)

Seeing Shouldn't Be Believing!

When George opened the front door of his house, his parents were on their way out. His father pointed to the message board next to the telephone. "Mario just called. He and Erica should be over here in about ten minutes."

"What about the snacks?" George asked. "I'm supposed to have them ready."

His mother pointed to the timer next to the stove. "When the timer goes off, everything will be ready. I didn't want the three of you to starve. Studying for a history midterm takes lots of energy."

"Thanks, Mom," George said.

"Hey, don't thank me. Thank your father. He makes a much better batch of nachos than I do."

"Just one thing, George," his father added. "Do you see how clean this kitchen looks?" George nodded. "Do you see how empty that garbage can is?" George nodded again. "When we get back from the movies, I'd like the kitchen to look the same way. And I want the garbage can to be empty, understand?"

"No problem, Dad," George answered. "Have a great time at the movies. And thanks for the nachos."

George dumped his backpack on the sofa and set up to work. Within 15 minutes, his history books were piled on the dining-room table. He was just setting out the tray of nachos when the doorbell rang. It was Mario and Erica. George led them into the dining room while he brought out the chips and salsa.

Erica surveyed the books and pads of paper in disbelief. "I've never seen you this organized before," she said to George.

"I'm highly motivated," he answered. "The sooner we start studying, the sooner we can stop."

"And do some serious channel surfing," Mario added.

Erica shook her head. "Come on, guys. Get serious. I didn't come over here to hang out with two couch potatoes."

Mario pointed to the plate of nachos in the center of the dining-room table. "Me, neither. This is like a serious study night. If I don't ace this exam, my parents will kill me."

George, Erica, and Mario sat down at the table and opened their books. George looked at the remote control. Mario moved the bowl of chips closer to his hand. "Brain food," he said sheepishly when Erica looked at him.

She picked up a stack of note cards. "Ready, guys?" she asked. George and Mario looked at each other.

"Ready," they both answered.

Two hours later, the plate of nachos was empty and the wastebasket was full. George crumpled up one more sheet of paper, aimed at the basket in the corner, and scored a direct hit. "Well, that about does it." He checked his watch. "What about it, guys? We're just in time for 'My Life.' "

"What's that?" asked Erica.

George and Mario looked at each other in disbelief. How could anyone not know about "My Life"?

"Erica, my friend, there are some serious gaps in your education," Mario said.

"Fill me in. I'm willing to learn."

George turned on the TV. "This is only one of the best new shows on TV," he said. "It's about these nerds from another planet who move to Earth. Once they're here, they actually start looking like us. Get it?"

Erica stared at the TV screen. "I think so. But I'm still waiting to hear the plot."

Mario refilled the bowl of chips. "It's classic stuff. Once they look like us, they start acting like us. Then they enroll as students at some high school."

"Actually, some of the characters remind me of the kids in our class," added George. "Trust me. This is a totally cool program."

Mario pointed to the TV screen. "See that guy over there? He's the leader of the aliens. Last week, he was elected captain of the basketball team. Now all the other aliens have joined."

George howled with laughter. "The weird thing is they're all such terrific players. And they're from outer space."

"And," added Erica, "they're all men."

George passed a bowl of chips to Mario. "Wow!" Mario screamed. "That guy's unreal." He was pointing to one of the actors who had just scored a basket. "This is better than a real game at school. And look at those cheerleaders. Are they supposed to be aliens, too?"

George nodded. "I've been watching it since the first episode. You should have seen the show two weeks ago."

"I bet it was incredible," Erica said. She wasn't smiling.

"Exactly," George answered. "Here's the plot. See, the aliens had to learn how to dress like girls."

"Like women. We prefer to be called women," Erica added.

"OK, girls, women, whatever. The point is, on the show the aliens had to figure out how to dress like cheerleaders." He turned to Mario and Erica. "Get it? Like how to wear the cheerleading skirts and short boots. It was hysterical. In the beginning, they had to figure out how to put on makeup."

Mario pointed to the TV screen. "So all those cheerleaders are really from outer space. Man, I can really get into this show."

Erica picked up one of her textbooks and started

to read. "Sorry, guys," she said. "I don't want to interrupt your fun and games, but I thought I'd review the last chapter again."

Mario and George looked at each other and shrugged. "What's with her?" George asked.

"Maybe she just doesn't get it," Mario answered.

Erica slammed down the book. "No, she gets it all right. She just doesn't find jokes about cheerleaders and girls very funny. By the way, what was the name of that cheerleading squad, anyway?"

"It was called 'The Babes,' " answered George.

Erica grabbed the remote control from George's hand. "Somehow that doesn't surprise me," she said.

"Hey, what are you doing?" asked Mario.

"Trying to find something we can all watch," she answered. George and Mario slumped back in their chairs. 'My Life' disappeared from the screen. Scenes from a variety of shows flashed by. A scene in a supermarket was replaced by a scene in a shopping mall. The shows flew by so rapidly, all the faces started to blur.

George grabbed for the remote control, but Erica refused to give it up. "Wait a second," she said. "Molly told me about this show last week. It's about some people who live in the same apartment building."

Erica settled back in her chair. George looked at Mario with a "What's the use?" expression. The boys looked at the TV screen. Neither laughed. "This isn't funny at all," George said.

"What do you mean, not funny? This show's terrific. The guys are being real nerds in the kitchen. See, they don't even know how to turn on a stove or make coffee. Typical." Erica started to laugh.

"Wait a minute," said George. "That's not typical at all. How did you like those nachos?"

"I loved them," Erica answered.

"Glad to hear it. I'll have my father give you the recipe. He made them."

Mario gave George the high-five sign. "Way to go, man. See, Erica, you think the show's funny. Well, we think it's sexist."

"OK, OK. That's one small example," she said. She pointed to the screen and started to laugh. "Come on. Look at those two guys trying to feed the baby. I mean, they don't have a clue about what to do."

Mario took out his wallet and pointed to a picture. "What do you think of her?" he asked Erica.

"What a terrific kid. How old is she?"

"Just turned four years old. Her name's Rosalie. I've been helping take care of her since she was born. She's my baby sister." He pointed to the TV screen. "You think that's funny? Well, I'm not laughing."

George took the remote control from Erica. The screen went blank. All three looked at one another uncomfortably.

"Face it, guys," George said. "There're a lot of stereotypes on TV."

"And a lot of them are sexist," Erica added. "Do you think there's anything we can all watch and enjoy?"

"I have an idea," said George. "We channel surf for a full minute, and the first show that looks good, we . . ." Mario, George, and Erica were startled by the sound of the front door opening.

"My parents," George said. He turned off the TV and put away the remote control. "We forgot to clean up the kitchen. Erica, you take out the garbage. Mario and I will start on the dishes."

"You see," said Erica. "I knew we could do something about those sexist stereotypes."

"I just didn't think it would happen quite this way," said Mario as he picked up a kitchen towel and got to work.

Lesson 1:
Distinguishing Between Fact and Opinion

When people are trying to influence you, they often state their opinions as if they were facts. An advertisement for breakfast cereal, for example, doesn't say, "I *think* Macho Cruncho is the most nutritious and best-tasting cereal. I don't *believe* you can buy a better cereal for the money." Instead, that opinion is made to sound like a fact: "Macho Cruncho is without a doubt the most nutritious, best-tasting cereal money can buy!"

It's easy to accept such statements as fact and to let someone else form your opinions. How can you guard against this? Be a critical listener and a critical reader. Don't believe everything that you see and hear.

What is the difference between a fact and an opinion? A fact can be tested or proved to be true or false. An opinion is what someone thinks or feels about something. It's what someone believes to be true, but it cannot be tested or proved. Other people may disagree with it and have a different opinion.

For example: Paco scored 23 points in last night's basketball game. (Fact) Paco is Northside's best athlete. (Opinion)

The following quotations have appeared in the media. Some of them are fact; some are opinion. Decide whether each one can be tested and proved to be true or false. If so, it's a fact. If not, it's an opinion. Think critically about each item below. Write either *Fact* or *Opinion* after each one.

1. "I don't know the key to success, but the key to failure is trying to please everybody." *Bill Cosby* __________

2. "Computers are useless. They can only give you answers." *Pablo Picasso* __________

3. "The human body contains 206 bones; women do not have one more rib than men." *Claudia Bowe* __________

4. "Television deprives children of their imaginations." *Theodore Isaac Rubin, M.D.* __________

5. "Winning is not everything. It's the only thing." *Vince Lombardi* __________

CHECKING FACTS

In common speech, we often use the word *fact* to mean "true." We say "That's a fact" to mean "That's the truth." In examining the misuse of language, however, we use *fact* to mean a statement that can be tested or proved to be *true* or *false*. Thus, statements of fact need to be checked to see whether the information they give is accurate.

Many publishers employ "fact checkers" to make sure the facts being presented are accurate. What appears to be a fact, however, may be incorrect. For example, suppose you wrote, "The Sears Tower is 312 stories tall." That statement is not an opinion. However, it is an incorrect fact. The Sears Tower is really 110 stories tall. As a critical thinker, you must watch out for incorrect facts. You must also be on the lookout for opinions that are stated as facts, such as, "The Sears Tower is a safer building than the World Trade Center."

Facts can be checked. Opinions need to be *evaluated* to see if they are reasonable or not. Opinions are more apt to be reasonable if they have facts to support them. For example, the fact that Paco scored 23 points in one game supports the opinion that Paco is Northside's best athlete.

Each statement below is either a fact or an opinion. In the blank after each number, write either F (Fact) or O (Opinion). Under each fact, tell what source you could use to prove the statement. (e.g., newspaper, encyclopedia, almanac.) Under each opinion, write a fact to support that opinion.

1. La Toya Jackson was born in Gary, Indiana. ______________

____

2. The flag of the United States is a beautiful and meaningful symbol of this nation. ______________________________

____

3. Vermont is called the Green Mountain State. ______________

____

4. Whoopi Goldberg's real name is Caryn Johnson. ____________

____

5. *People* is America's most interesting magazine. ____________

____

____

6. City real estate taxes went up 2 percent last year. ____________

____

____

You may decide to agree with someone's opinion, especially if that opinion is supported by facts. By using your critical thinking skills, you decide whether to agree or not, instead of blindly accepting someone's opinion as fact.

Facts are valuable. So are reasonable opinions. You have opinions about many things, such as sports, music, clothing styles, movies, and people, to name a few. How reliable are your opinions?

Test one of your opinions, using the following graphic organizer. In the box at the bottom, write the opinion that you want to test. In the boxes at the top, write facts that support your opinion. Boxes for four facts are given. If you can't think of at least two, test a different opinion.

Facts in the Almanac

A world almanac is one of the most useful fact-checking books available. It covers everything from the price of postage stamps to a condensed history of the world from 4000 B.C. to the present. The following is a small sampling of the many thousands of facts that you can check in an almanac:

- ❑ Oscar winners,
- ❑ inventor of the zipper
- ❑ governor of Iowa
- ❑ mileage between Detroit and Houston
- ❑ population of Honolulu
- ❑ date of next total eclipse
- ❑ Daytona 500 winners
- ❑ location of Zaire
- ❑ copyright laws
- ❑ recent earthquakes
- ❑ complete Constitution of the United States
- ❑ Chinese calendar
- ❑ national parks
- ❑ unemployment insurance
- ❑ words to the National Anthem
- ❑ metric weights and measures

Supporting Facts

+

Opinion

DISCUSSION

If you met a famous major-league shortstop, would you ask his opinion on how to get a bank loan? Probably not. Most likely, you would talk about his specialty—baseball. Yet TV commercials often feature athletes who give their opinions on a variety of goods and services, including bank loans, soft drinks, and 900 numbers. Why are athletes commonly chosen as spokespeople for commercials?

Discuss why people are influenced by celebrities' opinions and how you can judge whether someone's opinion on a subject is reasonable. Give examples from the media.

Evaluation

Use the following questions to help you evaluate your performance on this lesson.

- ❑ Which statements gave me the most trouble in deciding whether they were facts or opinions? Why?
- ❑ What process did I use to validate opinions with facts?
- ❑ Do I think that what I learned in this lesson will help me in my own life? Why or why not?

Lesson 2:
Comparing the Emotional Effect of Words

Which would you rather be, amusing or silly? youthful or childish? daring or reckless? easygoing or careless? uninformed or ignorant? average or mediocre? inactive or lazy?

Each pair of words above has the same, or almost the same, meaning. Yet the feelings associated with them are different. The first word in each pair is associated with positive or neutral associations. *Neutral* means that the word does not influence feelings one way or another. The second word in each pair carries negative, or unpleasant, associations.

When people want to influence you, they choose their words carefully. If they want you to feel good about something or to support an idea, they choose words associated with positive feelings. Merchandise is not "overpriced" but "valuable." Wages that are offered are not "high" but "competitive." On the other hand, competitors' products are not "less expensive" but "cheap." Opponents do not "disagree" with their opinions but are "radicals" or "cranks."

It's important to be alert to this kind of language abuse so that you don't unknowingly allow someone else to mold your thoughts and opinions. You can detect such abuse by applying your critical-thinking skills and becoming a critical listener and critical reader. Practice those skills now. Use the graphic organizer on the next page to compare word meanings and the feelings associated with these meanings.

Begin by reading each list of words below. Decide which words are negative and which are positive. Write the three negative words from each list in the top half of the diagram. Write the three positive words from each list in the bottom half. You may use a dictionary if you wish.

1. thin, scrawny, slender, bony, slim, skeletal
2. scent, smell, aroma, fragrance, stink, odor
3. stubborn, determined, pig-headed, obstinate, unflinching, steadfast
4. confident, fanatic, unhesitating, certain, conceited, arrogant

DOUBLESPEAK AND EUPHEMISMS

Doublespeak is meant to mislead the audience. For example, a business that advertises "genuine faux diamonds" (*faux* is French for "fake") is selling "genuine" fake diamonds. The following are two examples of doublespeak because they are trying to hide what they actually are.

- ❑ nonmulticolor capability (black-and-white TV)
- ❑ hexiform rotatable surface compression units (steel nuts)

Euphemisms are different from doublespeak. The term *euphemism* comes from a Greek word meaning "good words." A euphemism is a pleasant or mild word used in place of what may be perceived as an unpleasant or negative word. The following are several examples of euphemisms:

- ❑ pass away (die)
- ❑ under the weather (sick)
- ❑ senior citizen (elderly person)
- ❑ restroom or lounge (toilet)
- ❑ action oriented (aggressive)

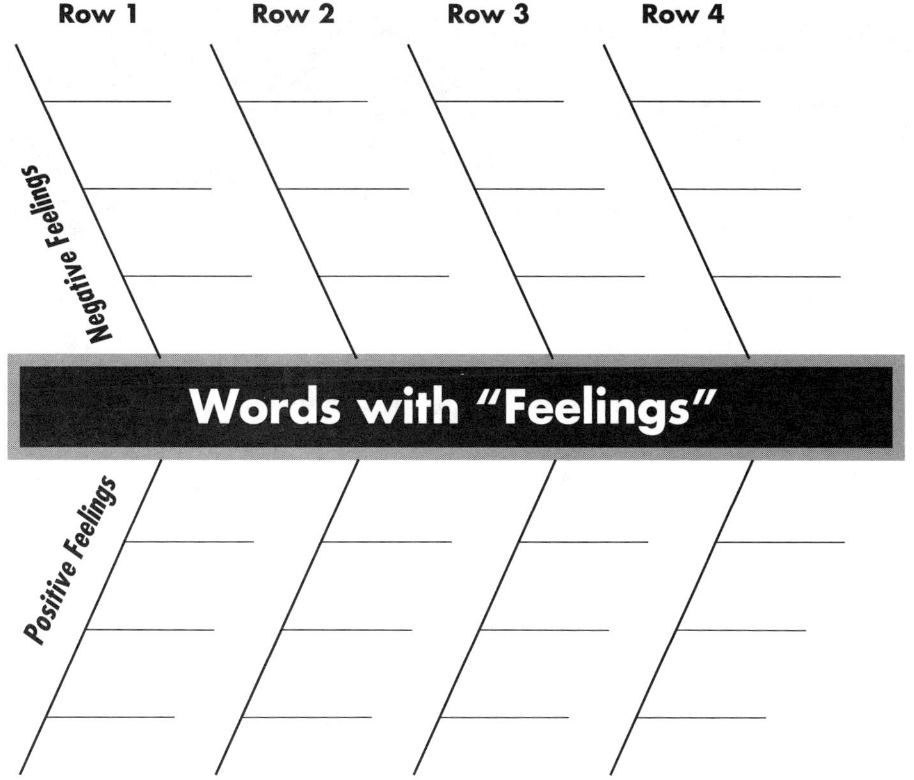

Words and phrases can be chosen to mislead the reader or to cover up unpleasant facts. This misuse of language is called "doublespeak." In "doublespeak," for example, a neutron bomb is called an "enhanced radiation device." This meaningless term is a more positive term because of the word *enhanced*. In addition, the word *device* replaces the negative word *bomb*. But this term hides the truth behind the devastating power of the "device." Examples of "doublespeak" are italicized in the sentences below. After each sentence, write a synonym for the italicized words and phrases. Choose from those listed below. Then write a sentence in which you use the new word.

prison taxes death failure

1. The rescue mission was an *incomplete success.* ____________

____

2. We are planning new *revenue enhancements.* ____________

____

3. The *negative patient outcome* is being investigated. ____________

____

4. He spent three years in *a correctional facility.* ____________

____

BOOKSHELF

You can find many resources in a library or bookstore about the use and misuse of language. The following are just a few of the books that are available. Check with your teacher, librarian, or a local bookstore owner for more titles.

What I Tell You Three Times Is True, by Jessica Davidson.

The Gender Trap: A Closer Look at Sex Roles, by Carol Adams and Rae Laurikietis.

Evaluation

Use the following questions to help you evaluate your performance on this lesson.

- ❑ Did the graphic organizer help me make comparisons? Why or why not?
- ❑ What process did I use to compare words and to associate them with either positive or negative feelings?
- ❑ How does what I learned in this lesson apply to what I see on TV and what I read in newspapers and magazines?

Lesson 3: Identifying Sexist Language and Stereotypes

One of the most harmful misuses of language is to stereotype people—to imply that all people in a certain group are alike (often in an unfavorable way) and have no individuality. Sexism is a form of stereotyping, as when someone says, "That's just like a man (or woman)!" Do you know anybody whom you would call a Yuppie? a preppy? a nerd? Those slang terms are all stereotypes that do not allow for a person's individuality.

A stereotype can be positive—but it's still a stereotype: "African Americans have great musical talent." While it is certainly true that some African Americans have great musical talent, it is also true that some are tone deaf. This stereotype, like all stereotypes, just isn't accurate. Many stereotypes—even stereotypes of an apparently positive kind—help to create prejudice. They blind you from seeing people as individuals.

Explain what the stereotype is in each of these sentences.

1. Your Irish temper is showing!

___

2. Stop crying, Brucie. Boys don't cry!

___

3. Kevin won't be any fun. He's a brain!

___

4. Headline: Housewife to Run for Mayor

___

5. You can't trust him. He's a politician.

___

Sexist language is an issue because it is a subtle way of stereotyping people and putting them down—from the time they are old enough to talk. In English, most sexist language works against women because the English language tends to favor men. The pronouns *he* and *him* have been commonly used to refer to both men and women. Sexist: "To boldly go where no man has gone before." What does such a sentence imply about women? That they don't count? That they aren't adventuresome?

CORRECTING SEXIST LANGUAGE

The following examples include suggestions on how to correct sexist language.

- ❑ early man (nonsexist: early men and women)
- ❑ homeowner and his wife (nonsexist: homeowners)
- ❑ lady professor (nonsexist: professor)
- ❑ fair sex; weaker sex (nonsexist: women)
- ❑ congressmen (nonsexist: members of Congress)
- ❑ businessmen (nonsexist: businesspeople, businesspersons)
- ❑ the common man (nonsexist: ordinary people)
- ❑ gal Friday (nonsexist: assistant)
- ❑ old wives' tale (nonsexist: story, superstitious belief)
- ❑ the ladies chattered (nonsexist: the women talked)
- ❑ *women's lib* (nonsexist: women's movement)
- ❑ *women's libber* (nonsexist: feminist)

The following are more examples of sexist language. On the lines below each item, write a nonsexist word or phrase to replace the sexist language.

1. starlet

nonsexist: ______________________________

2. workmen, policeman

nonsexist: ______________________________

3. mankind

nonsexist: ______________________________

4. girls, gals, ladies

nonsexist: ______________________________

Underline each example of sexist language or other stereotypes in the sentences below. Then rewrite the sentence, eliminating that misuse of language.

1. How did prehistoric man discover fire?

____

2. Jennifer is the chairman of the Committee on Doublespeak.

____

3. Everyone must sign his application and give it to Miss Gray.

____

4. Let's go Dutch Treat. We'll each pay our own way.

____

DISCUSSION

What are some stereotypes about teens? Have you ever heard adults say, "All teens are self-centered!" Do you agree with this stereotype? How does the stereotype make you feel? How would you refute this stereotype?

How do you think stereotypes got started? Is there any truth in them? How do stereotypes prevent critical thinking? How do you suggest dealing with stereotypes?

THE MATTER OF MS.

Women have pointed out that *Mr.* does not indicate whether a man is married. *Mrs.* and *Miss*, on the other hand, indicate marital status. Because of this difference, a movement in favor of Ms. began in the 1970s. *Ms.*, its backers say, helps to equalize the status of men and women. *Ms.*, like *Mr.*, is neutral concerning marital status. People in business generally like the idea. It allows them to address a woman as *Ms.*, either in person or in writing, without having to know whether she is married. By the way, *Ms.* can also be spelled *Ms* (without the period). Both forms are acceptable.

Evaluation

Use the following questions to help you evaluate your performance on this lesson.

- ❏ What process did I use to identify sexist language and stereotyping?
- ❏ How will I apply what I learned in this lesson in everyday life? Do I encounter sexist language or stereotypes in my day-to-day activities? Explain.

Reporting the News: "Language Abuse Exposed!"

Throughout this unit, you have been thinking critically about an important issue, the misuse of language that wrongly influences people's thoughts, feelings, and actions. In Lesson 1, you distinguished between fact and opinion. In Lesson 2, you compared the emotional effect of words by identifying words with either negative or positive associations. In Lesson 3, you identified sexist language and stereotypes. You have become sensitive to language abuse. You have learned how to spot such abuse and how to protect yourself from it. Now you'll have a chance to apply what you have learned in real-life situations.

Working as a reporter for a TV news program your assignment will be to uncover the ways in which language is misused in the media in order to trick an unwary public. You'll identify opinions stated as though they were facts, words chosen for their emotional appeal to deceive the public, sexist language, and language that promotes stereotypes.

When you have gathered your facts and examples, you will meet in small groups to prepare a story for a TV news broadcast. Each group will produce one segment of the show, while the rest of the class will play the TV viewing audience. After each segment, the audience will "call in" their comments and questions to the TV reporters.

As a reporter for the "Language Patrol," you will meet the issue of language abuse head on, and you will discover its importance—how it affects you and society.

STEP 1 Brainstorming and Planning

Imagine yourself now as a reporter on the Language Patrol. Your job is to root out misuses of language wherever you find them and to report the worst cases to your TV-viewing public. Where should you start your investigation?—TV? radio? newspapers? magazines? Think about likely places to spot language misuse. Make a cluster map to help you record your ideas quickly. A sample map is started below. Add additional clusters and branches as necessary.

Next, mark the most likely sources of language misuse. Then prioritize the sources. Number your choices 1, 2, 3, and so on, to plan the order of steps you'll take as you seek to uncover language pollution in the media.

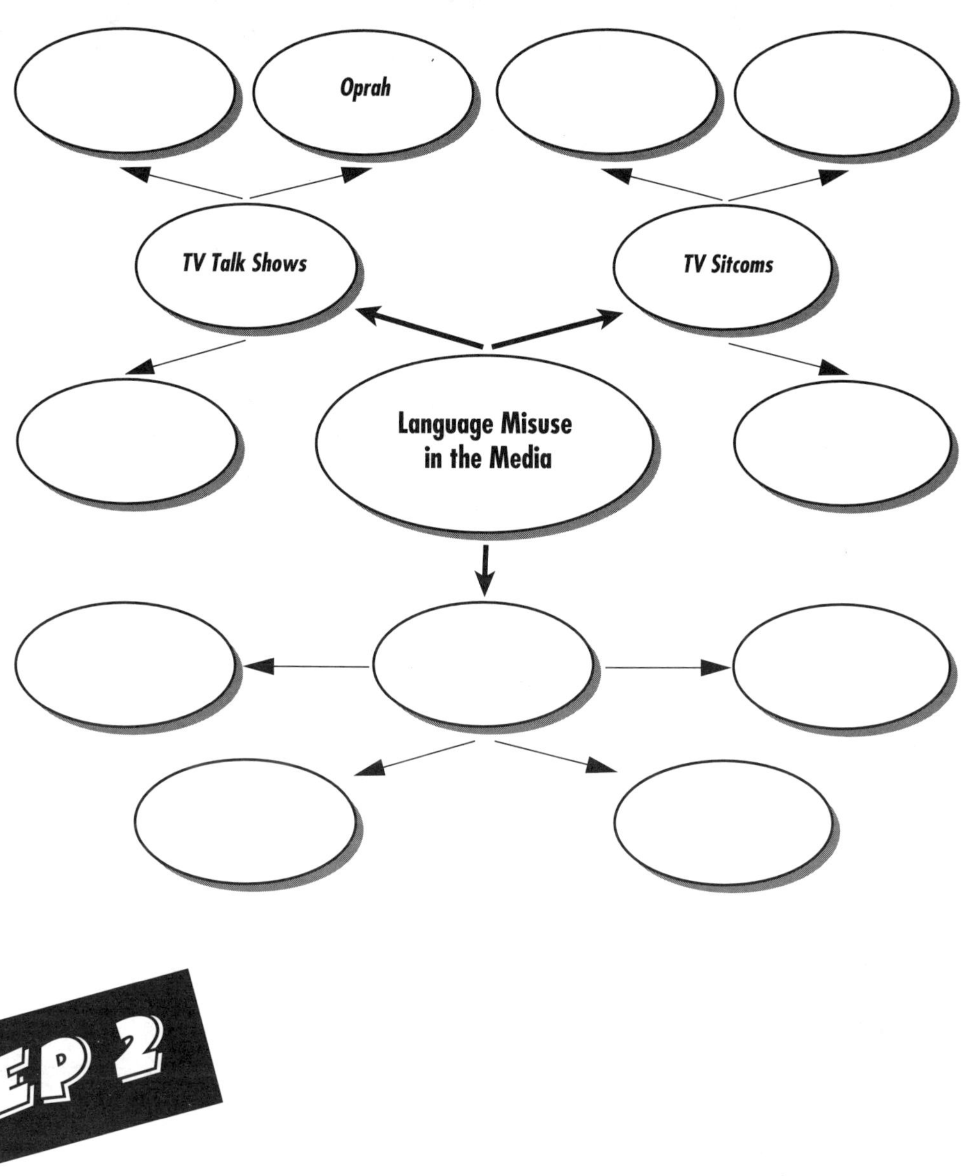

STEP 2

Gathering Facts and Examples

Follow the plan you've developed to gather examples of how language is being misused in the media. As you listen and watch, jot down your notes and examples.

Afterward, fill in details, such as the name of the TV or radio program and who said what. As you look through newspapers and magazines for examples, cut them out or photocopy them. Otherwise, copy the example and note the name, date, and page number of the publication from which it came. Or note the name of the TV or radio program and the date on which it was aired. Then bring your examples to class.

STEP 3

Planning a Presentation

Get together with a small group of students and share the examples you've collected. Discuss them and get your classmates' opinions on which ones are the best examples of language misuse. Narrow your choices down to two or three. Then together plan your group's segment of the TV news broadcast. Decide as a group which example each person will present, keeping in mind that you'll want to show a variety of examples and will want to present different kinds of language abuse. Use the chart below to help you. Next to each kind of language abuse, write the name of the student or students who will present each example.

Stating Opinion as Fact:

Using Emotional Words to Deceive the Public:

Using Sexist Language:

Using Language that Promotes Stereotypes:

Decide how much time each person will have to present an example. Then work individually to write your scripts.

Rehearsing

Meet with your group to rehearse your portion of the show. Choose someone to act as your TV anchorperson. That person will introduce your presentations to the TV audience (your classmates) and will supervise "phone calls" from TV viewers after everyone has finished. Rehearse your presentations. Appoint a timekeeper to give each person a signal when time is about up.

Afterward, discuss how you can improve your presentations. Prepare any audiovisual material, such as charts, pictures, diagrams, and so on, that you may want to use to illustrate your points.

Broadcasting the News

The time to broadcast the news has arrived. Before you begin, decide as a class which group will go first, second, and so on. Then start the show!

When you are in the TV-viewing audience, listen carefully and take notes on any questions that you have. If you have a question or comment, "call it in" when the anchorperson asks for phone calls.

STEP 6 Evaluating Your Presentation

As a group, evaluate your performance by answering the following questions:

- Was the show interesting?
- Was it informative?
- What did we learn from the experience of being investigative reporters tracking down language abuse?
- What did we learn from the experience of planning and participating in a TV news broadcast?
- How can we apply what we have learned in our everyday life?

1. Write the kind or kinds of language abuse each sentence contains and explain your answer. Choose from among the following: *stating opinion as fact, using sexist language, deceiving with emotional words, promoting stereotypes.*

a. All men are created equal.

b. Of all breeds of dogs, the Rottweiler is the most noble.

c. Only the English could enjoy a dull game like cricket!

____

____

____

____

____

____

Answer the following question on the lines provided. Use examples and details to support your answer.

2. Why is it important to distinguish opinions from facts? What can happen if you don't?

____

____

____

____

____

____

? Answer the following essay question on a separate sheet of paper. Support your answer with examples and details.

3. What would a society free of stereotypes and language misuse be like? Write a description of such a society. Explain how that society would be different from present society.

Unit 5

Becoming a Smarter Consumer

A recent survey revealed that 90 percent of all Americans have had some contact with telephone fraud. The survey showed that nine out of ten consumers have received offers from fraudulent telephone salespeople. Three out of every ten people—almost fifty-four million consumers—responded to fraudulent invitations.

Men and women who deliberately try to cheat people out of money, property, personal belongings, and so on, are called confidence men, or "con artists." They were given this name because these people artfully take people into their confidence before cheating, or "scamming," them. As your life changes and you become more independent, you can also become more appealing to con artists.

In this unit, you'll learn about some common scams and frauds that con artists pull on unsuspecting victims. In Lesson 1, you'll recognize deceptive practices and identify how they work. In Lesson 2, you'll learn to identify common telephone scams. In Lesson 3, you'll learn techniques to avoid becoming a victim of fraudulent schemes. In the unit project, you'll identify and report a consumer scam in your community.

Are You Gullible?

Would you fall victim to one of these schemes? This quiz presents four schemes. For each one, circle A, B, or C for the response that best describes how you would respond.

1. At two in the morning, your phone rings. A voice says, "Cousin Jake?" "Jimmy?" you mumble, half asleep. "Yes, it's me, Jimmy. I'm sorry to wake you up, Jake, but I have a problem. The police picked me up for speeding, and now I'm in jail. I need $200 bond money to get out. It'll just be a loan. I'll pay you back. My friend Lou lives near you. That's why I called you. He'll come over and pick up the money. Okay, Jake?"

a. You tell Jimmy that you're sorry about his problem and that you'll have the money ready.

b. You feel bad, but you don't commit to the money. You say you'll talk to Lou when he comes over.

c. You tell Jimmy you want to talk to the officer on duty. If you do post bail money, you'll come by later in the morning.

2. You're leaving the shopping mall when you see a car at the edge of the parking lot. The trunk is open and several people are there talking. You go over to see what's going on. The back of the car is filled with boxes carrying the name of a name-brand videocassette recorder. One of the machines is out of the box, and it looks real. "It is all top quality, new merchandise," the driver says. "But I can't stay here long." He looks around very nervously. Although you think the VCRs may be stolen property, you know the price is great.

a. You can't pass up this bargain. You agree on a price and hand over the money without looking in the box.

b. You tell the driver you need time, but he doesn't want to wait. Others are buying the machines, so you think it must be OK. You buy one, too, without looking at it.

c. You tell the driver you don't do business with stores that wear license plates. You walk away and call the police.

A woman offers to sell you a winning lottery ticket for half its cash value. She says that she cannot turn it in because she is an illegal immigrant and that she would be deported, or sent back to her country, if she tried. She offers you proof of the winning ticket number.

a. You check the ticket and it looks real. It's worth $500, so you give her $250, knowing you'll get $500 for cashing it in.

b. You say you won't buy the ticket, but you will cash it in for her. The woman agrees but asks if she can hold something valuable of yours until you bring her the money. You give her your watch to hold.

c. You tell her that you don't know whether the ticket is real or not. You walk away and call the police.

Your aunt died and the funeral is just over. The doorbell rings, and there's a messenger with a C.O.D. package addressed to your aunt.

a. Thinking it might be something valuable that your aunt ordered, you take the package and pay the C.O.D. charges.

b. You ask to see the item. It's a Bible. Thinking you would like something of your aunt's, you pay the charges.

c. You tell the messenger your aunt has died, so you cannot accept delivery of the package.

Scoring Your Answers

If you circled any A choices, you have just been swindled. See the details below. If you circled any B choices, you're cautious but still could be swindled pretty easily. If you circled the C choices, a con artist wouldn't get anywhere with you.

Behind the Schemes

1. **Bail-Bond Con:** The con artist drives through a neighborhood, choosing potential victims' addresses to telephone later. In the middle of the night, when most people are not clear thinking, the con artist calls. He also picks up the money, posing as a friend.
2. **Stolen Goods Scam:** The victim is led to believe the goods are stolen. When you get home, you discover you have a box of bricks. The swindler is gone.
3. **Lottery Swindle:** This swindle is becoming more and more popular. You lose two ways: the money that you give the woman and the problems that you have trying to cash a counterfeit ticket.
4. **Obituary Hoax:** The con artist identifies potential victims through the obituary column in the newspaper. He dresses up as a messenger and "delivers" a C.O.D. (collect on delivery) package containing an inexpensive item.

Thousands of people are the silent victims of con artists every week. But there is help available.

Where to Go for Help

The **U.S. Postal Service** investigates complaints about businesses that use the mail to advertise or sell fraudulent merchandise or investments. This activity includes telephone salespeople and newspaper advertisements because money sent in answer to them is usually mailed. Contact your local postmaster or the postal inspector in the telephone book under *U.S. Government, Postal Service.*

The **Food and Drug Administration (FDA)** investigates and prosecutes fraudulent misrepresentation and deceptive claims by food and health-product manufacturers. This agency has the power to force manufacturers to change labels and claims and to seize products if the company refuses to comply with its rulings. For information, write to the Food and Drug Administration, Washington, D.C. 20580.

The **Federal Trade Commission (FTC)** investigates complaints of advertising and investment scams. It cannot resolve individual complaints but uses the complaints to develop law-enforcement actions. Send complaints in writing to Correspondence Branch, Federal Trade Commission, Washington, D.C. 20580.

The **Alliance Against Fraud in Telemarketing** is made up of state, federal, industrial, and consumer groups, as well as trade unions and law-enforcement agencies. The alliance will forward your complaint to the agency responsible for investigating and prosecuting con artists. Write Alliance Against Fraud in Telemarketing, 815 15th Street NW, Suite 516, Washington, D.C. 20005.

The **Better Business Bureau (BBB)** will take reports about frauds and cons. However, they have no right to prosecute illegal operators. Contact the Better Business Bureau of the town or city in which a fraudulent company is located or call the Council of Better Business Bureaus at (703) 276-0100.

Local Telephone Companies have information about frauds that take place over the telephone. It will also assist in the investigation of fraudulent telemarketing practices. Contact your local telephone company.

The **Local Police Department** will investigate or take action against individuals accused of fraudulent practices. If you are a victim of a fraud within your community, contact the local police department to file a report or to request officers to go to the scene of the crime.

Lesson 1: Identifying Deceptive Practices

Confidence men, or "con artists," as they are called, need victims in order to succeed. Two of their favorite targets are the young and the elderly. There are a number of reasons why young people look good to a con artist. First, the con artist knows you're taking steps toward independence. You're eager to show your experience and decision-making skills. Second, you're vulnerable to "kindness" from strangers and eager to gain new experiences. To draw you into the deception, con artists depend on your eagerness.

How can you make yourself deception-proof or nearly deception-proof? The following is a crash course in con artistry. The goal is to become familiar with the faulty arguments and tricks that con artists use on young and old alike.

Chances are you have already been or will be invited to take part in the following scheme—maybe more than once. Study the scheme. Then answer the questions that follow. The scheme is called the Pyramid, and it will often involve money. A chain letter for money or gifts works this way. In order to work, a pyramid scheme depends on an expanding number of participants. The one who starts the scheme puts his or her name at the top of a list that is sent to five people. These five people put their names on the list and send money to the first person on the list. These people then send the list to five people, who get money from twenty-five people, and so on. The first few tiers of people usually get quite a lot of money before the pyramid and the scam break down.

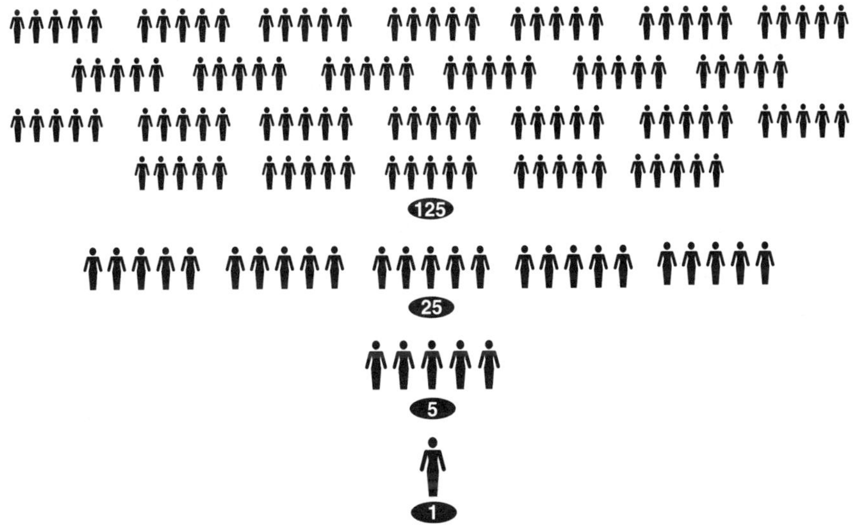

THE LANGUAGE OF THINKING

To recognize means to be able to identify an object or an idea. To recognize a scam, or a deceptive consumer practice, you must be able to recognize how the scheme works. Many con schemes are based on illogical or faulty reasoning and unethical practices. To be able to recognize such schemes, you need to be a thoughtful, critical, and wise consumer.

CONSUMER PROTECTION ACTIVITIES

Faulty or misleading advertising practices can also be a type of scam. The Food and Drug Administration (FDA) protects consumers from being cheated, misled, or otherwise deceived by manufacturers and advertisers of food and health products. If a manufacturer refuses to comply with the FDA's ruling about a deceptive label, the agency may seize the company's products to prevent their distribution. Recently, the FDA joined forces with the Federal Trade Commission (FTC), which controls advertising. These two agencies can protect consumers from deceptive advertising and sales practices.

Evaluation

Use the following questions to help you evaluate your performance on this lesson.

- ❑ Am I clear about some of the ways in which I may be vulnerable to cons? What are they?
- ❑ What strategy did I use to recognize how scams work?
- ❑ What are the ways in which I may be vulnerable to a scam's attractiveness?

1. If 125 people send in five dollars to the pyramid, how much cash has accumulated at this point?____________________

2. What makes this scheme deceptive?____________________

____

____

3. What other schemes are you aware of in which people lose their money in a situation that looks profitable? ____________________

____

____

____

The following is another popular scam. Read the following conversation that could take place in any public place or on the street. Then answer the questions that follow.

> "Please take this free book," a young woman said as I got out of my car. I told her that I was in a hurry and started to walk away. As I walked away, she followed me and showed me a current best seller. Being a book lover, I took it with a smile. "It's free," she said. "But I would ask for a small donation." I handed her twenty dollars and asked her for ten dollars in change. Even at ten dollars, I thought that I was getting a good deal. She gave me a ten-dollar bill and said, "Oh, that's my last ten-dollar bill. Tell you what. Give me back the ten-dollar bill, and I'll give you two five-dollar bills instead." She then rushed off to her next customer. By the time I got to my office and looked at what she had given me, I realized that she had folded up only one five-dollar bill instead of two.

1. How much did the person pay for the book? ____________________

2. Why did the scheme work for the con artist? ____________________

____

3. What other schemes are you familiar with in which people lose money because of faulty arithmetic? ____________________

____

____

Lesson 2:
Analyzing Telephone Scams

One former con artist said, "The telephone works beautifully for cheating people. It allows you to paint a picture that is not factual in the mind of a client. You couldn't do that face to face. The people who are responsible for making up our 'pitches' or for preparing our brochures create an illusion, and we paint that picture on the telephone."

Telephone con artists, also known as "yaks," are a close-knit community. They often work with one another, exchanging names of victims and other information. They know that once someone has been cheated, that person can probably be tricked again. The victim goes along again, hoping to regain his or her original loss. Some "yaks" claim to be able to cheat the same victim an average of six times.

Use the information above to complete the following statements.

1. The purpose of telephone scams is to ______________________________

____

2. Probably the reason people can be swindled more than one time is ____

____

3. Telephone scams work because______________________________

____

____

Most telephone scams are either for merchandise or investments. Most people can recognize an ordinary merchandise scam, such as one in which the caller says you've won a television set, but you must send $25 to cover shipping costs. (The TV is never sent, of course.)

A simple example of an investment scam is one in which the victim is offered an opportunity to buy gold at a discount of up to half the current market price. If the person sends money, he is called again and taken for all the money he or she has. (No gold is received.)

There are four questions you should ask yourself when talking with a telephone salesperson.

THE LANGUAGE OF THINKING

When identifying something, it is helpful to use criteria by which you can make an identification. To identify a scam and to recognize it as different from an ordinary telephone sales effort, for example, you should ask yourself the questions included in this lesson.

YAKETY YAK

Con artists who pull off telephone frauds have their own vocabulary.

Yak: A con artist who uses a prepared script to defraud someone.

Fronter: A yak who places the first call and makes the first sales pitch

Closer: A yak who closes the deal the fronter started

Mooch: A victim of a telephone fraud

Singer: A yak who tells the mooch how wonderful the product is

Reloader: A yak who makes a new pitch to someone who has already been the victim of a scam

TELEPHONE-SCAM FACTS

Currently, there are an estimated 265,000 businesses in the United States using the telephone to sell their products. Most are ethical. However, a growing number are not. Each year, there are more and more dishonest firms using the telephone to take people's money.

Telephone con artists swindle, or cheat, about 100,000 Americans every week, or about 10 Americans every minute. These con artists talk consumers out of between $10 billion and $40 billion a year or about $7,500 every minute. These numbers are only estimates because many victims never report the crime. One survey estimates that only 31 percent of the people cheated actually report their losses. Therefore, the actual extent of telephone fraud is not known.

1. *Does the caller refuse to give me time to make up my mind?* Telephone salespeople use high pressure to convince you to make a decision. They want you to think the same deal won't apply tomorrow.

2. *Does the caller refuse to mail me any free information?* Questions can be answered if the caller simply mails you something in writing before you make a decision. If the caller is unwilling, be careful.

3. *Does the caller pressure me for my credit card or checking account number?* It is unwise to give out any number to a stranger.

4. *Do I have to pay to win a free prize?* If you have to pay, the gift isn't free. Remember, you rarely get something for nothing.

The following is the script of a very common telephone scam. With a small group, analyze it, using the questions above and those below.

> *Hello! Am I speaking to . . . ? Good! Congratulations! You are the lucky winner of an all-expense-paid vacation to Hawaii. No, there's no mistake. The trip is yours. You don't have to do anything or visit any place. Congratulations!*
>
> *Now we just need a little information from you. First, I need to confirm your address, telephone number, and social security number. Good. Aren't you excited? Now, your trip voucher is good from either New York or Los Angeles. So you'll only have to purchase your transportation to either city. We just need your credit card number. Thank you; that's great. You'll receive everything—information, hotel reservations, airline tickets, and all vouchers within a week. Have a wonderful time!*

1. Why might this sound like an exciting free prize? ____________

____

2. What did the "yak" ask for that the victim should not give?

____

3. Do you think this person actually went on the vacation? What do you think happened to the person's credit card number?

____

____

The following are summaries of two other common telephone scams. For each scam, tell what the "yak" appealed to and the mistake that the victim made. Tell what the victim should have done.

You get a phone call from someone who claims to be from the phone company. She wants to "verify" use on your calling-card number and asks for that number. The following month you see hundreds of dollars worth of calls on your telephone bill.

1. The "yak" appealed to ______________________________

2. The mistake that the victim made was to ______________________

____

3. The victim should have ______________________________

____

You get a phone call from someone who says that you've won a free prize, but shipping charges must be put on a credit card. You give the number, and the following month you find numerous unauthorized charges.

4. The "yak" appealed to ______________________________

5. The mistake that the victim made was to ______________________

6. The victim should have ______________________________

____

Working with a partner, make up a set of guidelines to help you avoid becoming a victim of telephone scams. Use the chart below to record your responses.

Tips for Avoiding Phone Scams

Always	Never

BOOKSHELF

You can find many newspaper and magazine articles about fraud in a library or bookstore. The following are a few of the resources that are available. Check with your teacher, librarian, telephone company, and post office for more resources.

Sting Shift: The Street-Smart Cop's Handbook of Cons and Swindles, by Lindsay Smith.

Get Real! A Student's Guide to Money and Other Practical Matters, by James Tenuto and Susan Schwartzwald.

Evaluation

Use the following questions to help you evaluate your performance on this lesson.

- ❑ What strategy did I use to distinguish a legitimate telephone salesperson from a con artist?
- ❑ Do I now have an appropriate technique for dealing with legitimate telephone salespeople? What is it?
- ❑ What process did I use to develop tips for avoiding telephone scams?

Lesson 3: Recognizing Fraud

Distinguishing requires you to recognize aspects of two or more ideas or objects so that you can tell them apart.

To avoid becoming a victim, you must be able to distinguish a con from a legitimate sales effort. In other words, you have to recognize the intent behind situations.

FRAUD VOCABULARY

Other words associated with "fraud" include the following:

cheat (noun or verb)

con (verb, noun, or adjective)

defraud (verb)

fraudulent (adjective)

hoax (noun)

scam (noun)

swindle (noun or verb)

victim (noun)

victimize (verb)

Fraud is the act or practice of cheating or tricking someone. In other words, actual fraud is not accidental or unintentional. Its intent and motivation are to deceive and to do harm. It is important to remember this definition when you are distinguishing a simple overstatement or exaggeration from actual fraud.

If you are offered a name-brand watch at a discount price, for example, you would need to analyze the situation. If you, in fact, get the watch that you expected, then it is a legitimate deal. But if the salesperson takes your money without giving you the watch, if you have to pay more for the watch than it's worth, or if you get a phony watch, you are the victim of fraud.

In a small group, discuss the following two sales situations. Describe what would have to happen to make each one fraudulent and what would have to happen to make each one legitimate. Be specific. Be sure that you clearly describe the intent of the deal.

1. You are offered cheap land for sale in a sunny location. You send in a down payment.

Fraudulent

____

Legitimate

____

2. You buy a new health-care product by mail. You send a check or money order with the order.

Fraudulent

____

Legitimate

____

The following are four frauds operating today. Study each one and identify the fraudulent intent. Circle the phrase that distinguishes the intent. Then write what a good critical thinker should do to avoid being swindled.

1. The Con:

An advertisement offers a low price to clean one or more rooms.

The Outcome:

The cleaner says that the carpet is too worn or dirty and charges more.

To avoid being swindled, ______________________________

____

2. The Con:

A home "inspector" checks plumbing, wiring, trees, and so forth, for problems.

The Outcome:

The "inspector" finds a serious problem in the furnace and says that the heat must be turned off until the furnace is fixed. The "inspector" offers to call a repair person who is cheap and fast. But the work that is done is shoddy and expensive.

To avoid being swindled, ______________________________

____

3. The Con:

A charity asks for a contribution.

The Outcome:

You find out that no such group exists.

To avoid being swindled, ______________________________

____

4. The Con:

A young person is selling magazine subscriptions.

The Outcome:

No magazines arrive. Money goes into the young person's pocket.

To avoid being swindled, ______________________________

____

AVOIDING SCAMS AND FRAUDS

The Federal Trade Commission (FTC) and the National Consumers League advise the following:

- ❑ If it sounds too good to be true, it probably is.
- ❑ Do not be pressured into buying anything.
- ❑ Invest only in business opportunities that you know about.
- ❑ Get all the information you can about a company, store, or salesperson.
- ❑ Always read the fine print before you sign anything.
- ❑ Don't give out your credit-card or telephone-card numbers to strangers.

Evaluation

Use the following questions to help you evaluate your performance on this lesson.

- ❑ What technique did I use to distinguish legitimate from fraudulent intent in a sales situation?
- ❑ What process can I use to avoid becoming a victim of consumer fraud?

Reporting a Community Scam

No one knows exactly how many people fall victim to deceptive schemes every day. The reason for this lack of data is that many victims remain silent because they're embarrassed about the crime. In addition, many people become victims a second or even a third time in an effort to recapture their initial loss. Talking about these crimes may help prevent other people from falling victim. Talking about the criminals is also an important way of exposing them.

In Lesson 1, you recognized deceptive practices and identified how they work. In Lesson 2, you analyzed several common telephone scams and how to ask questions about the sales pitches you hear. In Lesson 3, you distinguished between legitimate and deceptive sales efforts. With these skills, you may be able to avoid becoming a victim of common fraudulent schemes.

In this project, you'll work to uncover a fraudulent scam that is going on in your community. You'll report the scam and unveil the con artists who are pulling it off. As a result of your efforts, you'll encourage family and community members to become more intelligent and vocal consumers.

Getting Organized

You'll work in a group to gather information and report on your community's experiences with fraudulent schemes. To prepare for your first group meeting, think about the following questions. Make some notes. When you finish, get together with your group to share information.

1. What kinds of scams might be going on in your community? ______________________

____

2. What people or groups in your community might have unique or common experiences that could lead them to fall victim to frauds? ______________________

____

____

3. What and who are the expert sources of information in your community? ________

____

____

4. How can you find out about scams in your community? ______________________

____

____

STEP 2 Writing a Questionnaire.......

Work in your group to make a plan of action. There are people to call and questions to ask. Once you have identified potential victims, you need to find out what their experiences have been. For example, if you know that the elderly are likely victims in your community, you could contact a local senior-citizen group or center. Ask the person in charge for permission to have the members complete a questionnaire. You may need to divide your group in order to contact more than one place.

We will contact ____

____

Now write your questionnaire. Keep it short. Use the sample questions below as a guide for developing your own questionnaire. Don't require people to give their names. Ask only those questions that will get you the information that you need.

1. Have you been the victim of a deceptive sales scheme? Yes/No

2. Has anyone whom you know been the victim of a deceptive sales scheme? Yes/No

3. If you answered yes to either question, please briefly describe the experience.

____

____

____

Spend several days gathering information and having people fill out your questionnaire.

STEP 3

Summarizing Your Information..........

Once you have all the questionnaires filled out, summarize the information. Use the following diagram. Share the results with the whole class.

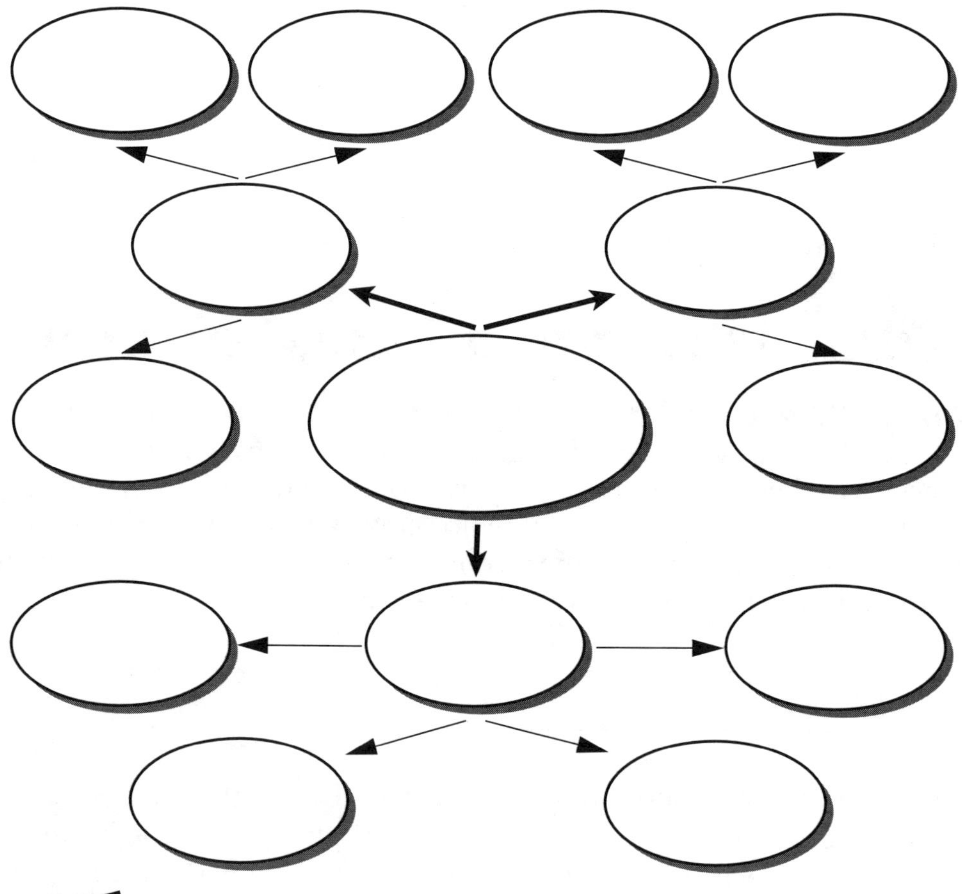

STEP 4

Planning a Report............................

Choose the scam that your group thinks is most important or harmful to the community.

Our scam report will be on ____

You'll present information about the scam in a television-like report. Choose a site where your report can take place and select one student to play each role (lead reporter, victims, authorities, and so on). Plan how your report will be sequenced, beginning with the lead reporter saying something like: "Good evening everyone. Our investigative team has uncovered a terrible scam in our community. We were very surprised to discover that . . ."

Write your report using the information you obtained from the questionnaire as evidence.

Practice your report. To be sure it is complete and objective, get together with your group and ask yourselves the following questions:

- Did we clearly describe how the scheme works? (In other words, did we give enough details so that people could recognize it if they heard or saw it?)
- If a special population was victim, did we clearly identify that population?
- Did we describe the scheme in a way that population can understand (appropriateness of language, examples, and so on)?
- If people gave details about the con artist, did we include those details (description of person, automobile, kind of letter he or she wrote, and so on)?
- Did we tell the people what to do if they are contacted by investigators (e.g., what they should say to the person who contacts them and whom they should call)?
- Did we verify that the authorities are aware of the scheme? Did we include what the authorities say people should do?

STEP 5 Presenting the Report

Give your report to the class, and—if possible—present it to the local media for follow-up. Give the scam as much publicity as possible to prevent it from spreading throughout the community. Be sure to let people remain anonymous for their protection.

STEP 6 Evaluating Your Report

Ask for feedback on your report. Remember that your goal was to help people in the community avoid becoming victims. With that goal in mind, invite comments from students, teachers, the media, and everyone whom you interviewed. Ask questions like the ones you used to check your group's report in Step 4.

1. Circle the phrase that best completes the following statement. Explain your choice. The important element in determining whether a sales technique is fraudulent is
   a. whether or not there is a victim.
   b. whether or not there is intent to harm.
   c. the judgment of the FTC or FDA.
   d. whether or not it is successful.

____

____

____

2. Put an X next to the statement that is true. Explain your choice on the lines provided.
   - ❒ Good critical thinkers are familiar with common scams and hoaxes.
   - ❒ Good critical thinkers know a strategy for asking questions.

____

____

Answer the following question, using details and examples to support your answer.

3. In this unit, you learned about many schemes, scams, and frauds. If you were to serve as a member of a community-action group to combat such practices, what would your contributions to the group be?

____

____

____

____

____

? Answer the following essay question on a separate piece of paper. Support your response with examples and details.

4. People over the age of 65 make up about 12 percent of the population. Yet they make up about 30 percent of the scam victims. What is it about the elderly and their lives that makes them so vulnerable to deceptive schemes? What can be done in your community to help the elderly avoid becoming victims of fraud?

UNIT 6

Teen Volunteers

Americans have a long history of volunteer service. They have always held the belief that one person can make a difference. In the 1960s, President John F. Kennedy made an appeal to Americans: “Ask not what your country can do for you; ask what you can do for your country.” His words changed and inspired many thousands of young people to help improve the lives of people in the United States and abroad.

More than 65 million people give their time to help others. Many are young people. In this unit, you’ll be shown how to become one of these volunteers. In Lesson 1, you’ll examine important social issues and weigh ideas about the kinds of work you could do as a volunteer. In Lesson 2, you’ll conduct a study of your community to see what is needed. In Lesson 3, you’ll propose a project that addresses an issue or a problem in your community. For the unit project, you’ll put a volunteer project into motion and you’ll see ways in which you can make a difference.

Reaching Out: Helping the Homeless

Tanya

Everyone in our school knew about the homeless shelters in our city. But the shelters weren't part of our lives in any way. That changed the day a fire destroyed one of the shelters. It was all over the local news that night. Once again, the homeless were without shelter.

A television news reporter interviewed the head of the shelter, Mr. Dworkin. He talked about the supplies they needed to reopen the shelter. Then he explained what the shelter did for the homeless every day. It provided a lot more than just food and clothing.

After hearing the interview, some of the students in my high school decided to help out. While the shelter was being rebuilt, the homeless people were staying in a nearby community center. But the staff there really wasn't equipped to take care of the homeless.

One of our teachers called Mr. Dworkin and asked him what students from his school could do. The next day, we posted a sign-up sheet on the bulletin board. By the end of the day, there were 40 names on the list.

We divided ourselves into groups. Some of us started a drive to collect sleeping bags and clothes to replace the items that had been destroyed in the fire. Another group went down to the community center every morning to help serve breakfast. Some students volunteered to serve dinner at the center a few nights a week.

After the shelter was rebuilt, we didn't stop. We couldn't. Instead, we thought about other ways in which we could help the homeless. Some students volunteered to help the shelter staff for an hour every day after school. Since more people were coming into the shelter, the people who worked there needed all the help they could get. We helped them contact city agencies that could provide housing. Sometimes, we took people to clinics for medical treatment.

We wanted to help the kids at the shelter, too. Some of them had missed so much school that they couldn't possibly keep up. A couple of students and teachers decided to start a special tutoring program for them. We all ended up doing a lot more than reviewing math or helping them with their reading. We became older brothers and sisters.

When I think about what we've done, I don't know whom we helped more: the people at the shelters or ourselves. I don't think that any of us look at this as some kind of "cause." For the first time, we think of the homeless as real people, not as a social problem that won't go away. Helping them is very important to me.

Juan

When I met some of the kids from my high school at the homeless shelter, I was already serving breakfast there three times a week. For me, it meant getting up an hour early every day. For the people who came to the shelter, it meant having a hot meal at the start of each day. That's something that all of us probably take for granted. Some of the homeless people told me that it was often the only meal that they had. I guess I was so used to knowing there would always be food in our refrigerator at home that I never imagined having to go without it or having to worry about where I would get my next meal.

I knew that the shelter could feed more people who lived on the streets. The kitchen was large enough. There were enough volunteers. What we really needed was the food. It seemed so unfair to me. There was all this food in restaurants, supermarkets, and bakeries. But sometimes there wasn't enough at the shelter, where people really need it.

Sometimes my mom and I eat at a restaurant near our apartment. One night, I asked the owner of the restaurant if he'd be willing to donate leftover food to the shelter. He told me that he had no problem with that. He had good food left over in the kitchen every day. It was a real shame to throw it away. He had thought about donating the food to a homeless shelter, but he never knew the right person to contact. Boy, was I glad I had talked to him.

The next day, I talked to our faculty adviser, Mr. Gonzalez. He'd been helping our group organize the volunteers at the shelter. He helped me plan a way to pick up leftover food from restaurants, bakeries, and supermarkets in our community. I was surprised by how many restaurants and stores were interested in helping us.

Getting places to donate the food was one thing. Getting the food to the shelter was something else. I've never been much for organizing, so I had a lot to learn. Mr. Gonzalez helped me plan a schedule of pickups and deliveries to the shelter and to another kitchen that feeds the homeless. At first, we used our parents' cars. Then a company donated a used delivery van that we could use. Now we can make our pickups and deliveries right on schedule.

I graduate this year, but I'm going to keep on volunteering at the shelter. It's made a big change in my life. I guess I appreciate what I have a lot more now. **And I can understand how important it is to be actively involved in helping people instead of just talking about it.**

FOOD DRIVE

Please bring a can or package of food to donate to the homeless shelter.

All donations will be collected in the cafeteria.

MAKING NEW FRIENDS...............

Douglas

For the past year and a half, I've been volunteering in an Elder Care program that was started at my high school almost five years ago. About thirty students are involved. Some of us spend one afternoon a week at a nursing home in our community. The rest are working with elderly people who live on their own.

What I find so terrific about volunteering at the nursing home are the friendships I've made with the people who live there. I wasn't sure at first whether I'd be able to handle going to a nursing home. To be honest, I didn't know what I'd say to a total stranger who might be frail or sick. But it wasn't that way at all. The very first afternoon I spent at the home, I talked with Mel, a 90-year-old man. He had the most amazing stories to tell me. When he was younger, he had been a sailor and had visited practically every country in the world. I couldn't believe how much he remembered. He really loved to play checkers, and he ended up beating me at every game.

I wasn't prepared for how interested the people in the nursing home were in the student volunteers. They wanted to know what we were learning in school and about our home lives, too. Because they were so much older, they sometimes had a different way of looking at things than we did. But you know something, that turned out to be OK. I think the kids who volunteered there got as much or more from the experience than the people whom they were helping.

When I told my social-studies teacher, Ms. Daley, about Mel and his stories, she suggested that I interview him for an oral history project about life in our city between the world wars. Other kids in the volunteer program were interested in the idea, too. The next week, I spoke to the director of the nursing home about the oral history project, and he thought it was terrific.

So did Mel and his friends. I think it made them feel important. They told us about events that we had only read about. Mel told me that it was the first time that someone had cared enough about his memories to interview him. I think it was his way of thanking me for becoming his friend.

I've been volunteering at the nursing home for almost a year now. I really look forward to the time that I spend there. It's made me understand how much people have to contribute at any stage in their lives. I've learned to be a better listener, and what I've heard has made a real difference in my life.

Lesson 1:
Examining Issues and Weighing Ideas

I used to say, "Just let me lead my life." But now I look around and see a world that needs me.

These are the words of a teen from Ohio who decided to get involved in what was going on around him. There are millions of people in America who need help. There are many teens who are helping out. Alone or in groups, young people are running recycling programs, staffing soup kitchens, and keeping senior citizens company. They are cleaning up schoolyards and parks. They are tutoring younger students or adults who need academic help. They are helping parents get their infants immunized from diseases, assisting at day-care centers, and being Big Brothers and Big Sisters. They are teaching children to swim and are coaching sports teams. The list goes on and on. But why? What might be some reasons that people volunteer their time to help others? Write your answer on the lines below.

To examine means to study something in all its parts, with a goal in mind. The goal might simply be to "see" something better, or it might be to understand something from a new perspective. The goal in examining social problems is to become better informed, to understand some of the causes of the problems, and to become involved in solving them. In examining options for volunteer work, the goal is to see the options from the perspective of your own needs and interests.

POSSIBLE REASONS FOR VOLUNTEERING

____

____

____

____

If you were to volunteer your time, how could you be most helpful? To make a wise choice, you would need to know what kind of work would be best for you. For example, do you want to work directly with people in need? Or would you be happier behind the scenes, helping out in an office, writing a newsletter, or organizing money-raising events?

The following questionnaire could give you some helpful information.

VOLUNTEER SELF-QUESTIONNAIRE

1. What three things do I perform well? ____________________

____

____

WHY VOLUNTEER?

According to a survey by Childreach, American teens are ready to take action even if it means making personal sacrifices. Volunteers say that they get involved for practical reasons. But what they get out of the volunteer experience is something else. They

- ❑ feel good about themselves
- ❑ get to know themselves better
- ❑ feel "empowered" (i.e., not helpless)
- ❑ feel they are part of life rather than observers of it
- ❑ feel happy doing something they choose to do

CURRENT SOCIAL ISSUES

- ❑ Homelessness
- ❑ Functional illiteracy
- ❑ Aging population
- ❑ Alcohol and drug abuse
- ❑ Environment
- ❑ Dropping out of school
- ❑ Teen pregnancy
- ❑ Violence among teens

2. What are three things that I enjoy doing? What are three things that I don't enjoy doing?

Enjoy	***Don't Enjoy***
____________________	____________________
____________________	____________________
____________________	____________________

3. What would I like to learn to do better? ____________________

____

4. What is an activity that I've never done but have always wanted to do? ____________________

5. Where do I like to be: indoors? outdoors? close to home? away?

____

6. Do I prefer being with other people or on my own? __________

____

7. What kind of people do I prefer to be with: older people? young people? people like me? people different from me? __________

____

8. Am I more comfortable working with groups or individuals?

____

9. What do I want to gain from volunteering? __________

____

10. Of all the problems that I see or hear about, which ones bother me most? ____________________

____

If you already have an idea for the volunteer activity that you might want to do, describe the activity on the lines below.

____

____

____

____

It's important to explore different options to see where you would be happiest and most helpful. Study the list of options for volunteer work below. Weigh each job honestly. Consider these two questions as you weigh each option:

- Why might this be a good job for me?
- Why might this be a difficult job for me?

In the following chart, write a brief reason for and against each kind of volunteer work.

JOB	MIGHT BE GOOD	MIGHT BE DIFFICULT
Working at a homeless shelter		
Tutoring homeless children		
Organizing a food drive		
Being an interpreter		
Tutoring adults		
Working for a charity		
Working at a senior center		
Helping an elderly person at home		
Being a peer counselor		
Giving talks about drugs		
Cleaning up a park or playground		
Organizing a recycling campaign		

Why is volunteer work important? What are the benefits of doing volunteer work for the volunteers themselves? for the ones receiving the help?

One of the most common excuses people have for not doing volunteer work is that they don't have enough time. What would you say to these people to convince them of the importance of doing volunteer work?

Evaluation

Use the following questions to help you evaluate your performance on this lesson.

- ❑ How easy or difficult was it for me to answer the questionnaire? Why?
- ❑ What did the questionnaire tell me about my own needs in connection with volunteering?
- ❑ How did I weigh options when I made decisions in this lesson? Why is it important to weigh one's options?
- ❑ How does the expression "One person can make a difference" apply to other areas of my life?

Lesson 2: Researching Community Needs

Finding the right volunteer opportunity can take a little time. Now that you know how to judge whether a volunteer opportunity might be right for you, you are better prepared to start your search. First, find out what your community needs. What are the organizations that need help? What community issues are crying for attention?

Make a list of the places, things, or people that you can think of that may need help. This list will help you know where to start looking.

_______________ _______________ _______________

_______________ _______________ _______________

Your community could be your school, neighborhood, city or town, or the whole country. You need to contact experts who can tell you which issues need attention and where the help is needed. Make a list of people whom you could visit, call, or write to get information. Remember churches, clubs, and town offices—anyplace where there might be someone who has information.

Contact Person	*Address, Phone Number*

Working in small groups, contact the people on your lists. But before you contact anyone, get organized. Be sure only one student from your group contacts each person. Know in advance what you want to say or ask. Tell the person whom you contact

- who you are and where you are from
- why you are contacting him or her
- what information you want

The following is one example of a polite contact. Plan yours to include the information that suits your purpose.

THE LANGUAGE OF THINKING

Researching means identifying and using expert help to find information. That expert help may take the form of books, journals, magazines, or other publications. It may also take the form of authorities, or expert people, with whom you might talk. In researching volunteer-job opportunities, people may be the best source of ideas. Publications may be the best source of names and addresses.

HELPFUL AGENCIES

ACTION is an agency of the federal government that coordinates nationwide volunteer activities, such as VISTA (Volunteers in Service to America). ACTION can provide information about various volunteer projects.

VOLUNTEER is a private organization that promotes volunteering nationwide. Its publications can provide information for volunteer centers in local areas.

Hello. My name is ____________. I am from __________ High School. I am calling you because my class is interested in volunteering our time for an important project in the community. Before we decide where we can be most helpful, I would like some information from you. Could you tell me, please, what you think are the areas of greatest need in our community? Can you tell me also the organization or person to contact to arrange our volunteer help?

Thank you very much for your help.

Set aside time every day to conduct your interviews. Use the following log to record the information that people give you. Don't be embarrassed to ask people to repeat phone numbers or to spell names if necessary.

Contact Log

Contact	*Information*	*Follow-up?*

Get together with your group. Share the information that you have gathered. List the job opportunities that each of you found.

Community Volunteer-Job Opportunities

BOOKSHELF

You can find many resources in a library or bookstore about volunteering. The following are just a few of the resources that are available. Check with your teacher, librarian, or a local bookstore owner for more resources.

Lend a Hand: The How, Where, and Why of Volunteering, by Sara Gilbert.

Volunteer! is a guide to opportunities for voluntary service. It focuses on work camps and overseas programs.

Evaluation

Use the following questions to help you evaluate your performance on this lesson.

- ❑ What process did I use to generate a list of volunteer-job opportunities in my community?
- ❑ What techniques did I use to interview people?
- ❑ What was the most difficult aspect of interviewing people? How did I overcome this difficulty?

Lesson 3:
Evaluating Volunteer Opportunities

There are many issues and needs facing American communities. All of them offer options for volunteer activities. But you can't do everything; you need to narrow your choices.

The following may be some of the issues your research showed to be important in your community. Read the list and check the issues you found to be important. Add any other topics you found that are not on the list.

Issue	In My Community?	Rank
health care	________	________
environment	________	________
youth violence	________	________
illiteracy in adults	________	________
reading problems of children	________	________
drugs or alcohol	________	________
teen pregnancy	________	________
HIV and AIDS	________	________
hunger	________	________
homelessness	________	________
animal care	________	________
arts and culture	________	________

____

____

____

Now rank the volunteer opportunities you found. Number the top four options in their order of importance to the community. The most important would be the one that the community needs most, or the one where there is an organization that needs the most help.

What are some specific jobs you could do to help in these areas? Work with a small group to brainstorm ideas. Write your job ideas on the following chart.

WHERE ARE THE VOLUNTEER JOBS?

Shelters. There are roughly 5,400 homeless shelters operating throughout the United States. Jobs at shelters include helping to cook meals, working in the office, and cleaning and making beds.

Feeding the Hungry. Volunteer activities to help feed the hungry include collecting food from stores and restaurants and bringing the food to soup kitchens and shelters. Volunteers are also needed at food banks for sorting and repackaging food that is donated by food manufacturers and grocery stores.

Tutoring. Most literacy centers allow high-school students to tutor adults or children on a continuing basis. Other jobs may include giving tests, helping with fund raisers, and recruiting volunteers.

Elderly. Volunteers are needed to work at senior centers, as well as in individual homes. Jobs may include shopping, reading, talking, and organizing activities.

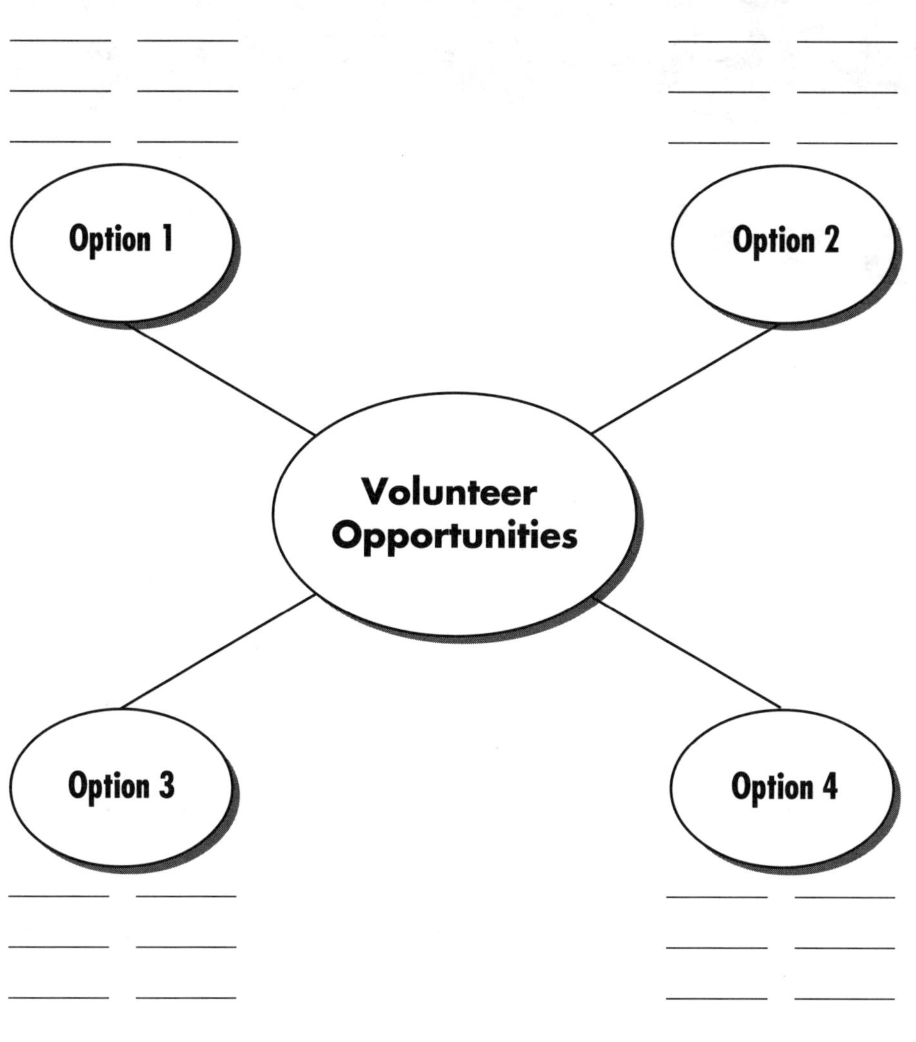

Examine the job ideas that you have for each issue and visualize yourself doing each job.

Your goal now is to select one volunteer job to recommend as your group unit project. Use the following criteria to evaluate the jobs for your final recommendation.

The following is a list of five criteria you should consider when evaluating whether a project would be appropriate. The project should be one that

- teens can do with little adult assistance
- will make a difference in the community
- can be ongoing, not a one-time event
- can be continued after school or on weekends
- does not require available resources and funds

Write your recommendation and give a reason for choosing it.

____

____

THE LANGUAGE OF THINKING

Evaluating means judging the value of an object or an idea. To judge something, you should use several criteria. Otherwise, judgments are merely opinions. In evaluating the volunteer-job opportunities in this lesson, use the criteria on this page.

Evaluation

Use the following questions to help you evaluate your performance on this lesson.

- ❑ What process did I use to rank ideas in order of importance?
- ❑ What strategy did I use to evaluate volunteer opportunities? How is this strategy useful in other subject areas?

Starting a Volunteer Project

Neighborhoods today are plagued by problems that have no quick and easy solutions. Malcolm X said that if an individual was not part of the solution, he or she was part of the problem. What he meant was that doing nothing makes you part of the problem. Becoming part of the solution means getting involved and making a commitment. By making a commitment, you can make a difference. One way to make a difference is by volunteering your time and energy for the good of people in need.

In Lesson 1, you learned about some social issues, and you analyzed the ways in which you might help most effectively. In Lesson 2, you researched the needs of your community and identified the places and people that need the most help. In Lesson 3, you evaluated several volunteer opportunities based on a set of criteria. Then you recommended one opportunity for your group to pursue.

In this project, you'll get the volunteer activity organized and put it into motion. You'll make a commitment to become part of the solution. In a short time, you'll see your efforts making a difference.

Making a Personal Commitment

Divide into groups according to the volunteer project you identified in Lesson 3.

Think about the kind of commitment you can make. Before you make a promise to anyone else, or to yourself, think about the following things. Make notes to take to the first meeting with your group.

Commitment Checklist

1. How many hours a week might I need to devote to this project? (Remember to include any travel to and from the place.) ______________________________

2. How much time do I have to devote to this project? (Remember school time, homework, any other activities you are committed to, as well as time for family and friends.) ______________________________

3. What hours do I have free? How flexible can these hours be?

   ____

4. How long a time can I devote to this commitment? (Set a reasonable length of time to be helpful, and know you can extend the time later.) ______________________________

   ____

5. Will it cost me anything to do this volunteer job? (Will you need travel money? money for a meal? any equipment?) ______________________________

Look over your answers and analyze them. Are the answers compatible with the needs of the volunteer job your group has selected? Why or why not? ______________________________

____

____

Take the time that you need to feel comfortable with your commitment to the volunteer activity. Once you are comfortable, get together with your small group. If you need to switch groups because you cannot commit to your group's choice, do so now.

Organizing a Group............

Decide whether you need a faculty adviser or sponsor.

You may also need community support for your project. In addition to consulting school resources, such as the principal and guidance counselor, you may need to seek out resources and support within the community.

Have a meeting with your group and talk about the project. Begin by discussing your answers to the Commitment Checklist. Do you all agree that the volunteer job is appropriate and one to which you can all commit? Then discuss the following questions:

- Why do we want to do this job?
- What can we do to help this cause?
- When can we do the job? For how long can we commit to it?

Recall the criteria for evaluating a volunteer opportunity (in Lesson 3). In particular, make sure the project you have chosen is one that teens can do, will make a difference in the community, and is ongoing and not a one-time event.

Make a "Jobs To Do" sheet. Assign responsibility for jobs to the individual group members. Write down any tasks that you need to do to get started. For example, do you need to contact people? Do you need to get any supplies? Will you make announcements? Use the chart below to help you to organize your project. It is set up for four group members, but you can combine people for tasks if your group has more than four members.

Volunteer Project Name ______________________

Purpose of project ______________________

____

Time Frame ______________________

Core group members

______	______	______
______	______	______

Tasks

______	______	______	______
______	______	______	______
______	______	______	______
______	______	______	______
Person Responsible	**Person Responsible**	**Person Responsible**	**Person Responsible**
______	______	______	______

You may also need a calendar for your project. Use a regular calendar with room in which to write activities and events.

STEP 3 Taking Action

Set time aside for your group to meet and begin your project. Do you need to meet with anyone else? Or can you just begin your project? The following is one example of a student project, with a description of how the volunteers got started.

A Beach Cleanup

Students from a school in Massachusetts observed that their local beach was strewn with litter and plastics. The sponsor, an assistant principal, put them in touch with the Metropolitan District Commission (MDC). That group was looking for students to get involved in its "Don't Trash Our Future" project. MDC officials met with the students and gave them Environmental Protection Agency checklists to use in their cleanup efforts. The students formed teams and went to work.

The students picked up more than 2,000 pieces of plastic, which they recorded. They wrote a paper for a press conference held by the MDC, and they made recommendations concerning the area's use of plastics.

Publicizing Your Experiences

Meet regularly with the class to report your experiences. Include your sponsor as well. You may wish to submit an article to your high school and community newspapers. You can also use the media to make appeals for assistance or to bring your project's needs to the attention of the public.

Evaluating Your Project

Meet regularly with your group to talk about how the volunteer project is going. Discuss ways in which you can be more effective. For example, would it be more helpful to spend more time or to spend it differently? Do you need anything to make your work more effective? If so, how could you get what you need? In addition to this evaluation, invite your sponsor or any adult involved with your project to give you feedback. For example, does the person think the project is going well? Does he or she think there are things you should do differently?

1. Circle the phrase that best completes the following statement. Explain your choice. Volunteerism in the United States is a response to

a. the Constitution of the United States.
b. the individual making a difference.
c. a difficult economic time.
d. community needs that arise.

2. Put an X next to the statements that are true. Explain your choices on the following lines.

❒ Critical thinkers weigh options that are available to them.
❒ Critical thinkers generate a lot of options to consider.
❒ Critical thinkers do not examine their own experiences in making decisions.

Answer the following questions, using details and examples to support your answer.

3. How can you apply the techniques you learned about weighing and evaluating options in your everyday life?

? Answer the following essay question on a separate piece of paper. Support your response with examples and details.

4. Some experts say that urban violence is a reflection of the conditions of the community. In areas where there are healthy activities for young people there tends to be little violence. The same experts also say that community problems can only be resolved when people become involved in their community. Do you agree or disagree? Why?